Otterville and Burgessville Ontario in Colour Photos, Saving Our History One Photo at a Time

Photography
by Barbara Raué
©2019

Series Name: Cruising Ontario

Book 242: Otterville and Burgessville

Cover photo: 244 Main Street East, Otterville, Page 27

©All the photos in this book have been taken with my cameras. I own the rights to them.

Series Name: Cruising Ontario, Saving Our History One Photo at a Time in colour photos

Books Available in Alphabetical Order:
Aberfoyle, Acton, Ajax, Alton, Amherstburg, Ancaster, Arthur, Auburn, Aylmer, Ayr, Beaver Valley, Belfountain, Belgrave, Belleville, Bloomingdale, Blyth, Brantford, Brockville, Burford, Burgessville, Burlington, Caledon, Caledonia, Cambridge, Carlow, Cayuga, Chatsworth, Cheltenham, Clifford, Colborne, Collingwood, Conestogo, Delhi, Dorchester to Aylmer, Drayton, Drumbo, Dundas, Dunlop, Dunnville, Eden Mills, Elmira, Elora, Embro, Erin, Essex, Fergus, Fort Erie, Georgetown, Goderich, Grimsby, Guelph, Hagersville, Haldimand County, Hamilton, Hanover, Harriston, Hespeler, Ingersoll, Inglewood, Innerkip, Jarvis, Kingston, Kingsville, Kitchener, Lake Superior, Lincoln, Linwood, Listowel, London, Lucknow, Merrickville, Mono, Mount Brydges, Mount Forest, Mount Pleasant, Neustadt, New Hamburg, Newboro, Newport, Niagara-on-the-Lake, Niagara Falls, North Bay, Oakville, Onondaga, Orangeville, Orillia, Oshawa, Otterville, Owen Sound, Palmerston, Paris, Parry Sound, Pelham, Perth, Peterborough, Petrolia, Pickering, Port Colborne, Port Elgin, Port Hope, Port Perry, Portland, Preston, Rockwood, Sarnia, Sault Ste. Marie, Seaforth, Sheffield, Shelburne, Simcoe, Smiths Falls, Smithville, Southampton, St. Catharines, St. George, St. Jacobs, St. Marys, St. Thomas, Stoney Creek, Stouffville, Stratford, Strathroy, Sudbury, Tavistock, Terra Cotta, Thamesford, Thunder Bay, Tillsonburg, Toronto, Uxbridge, Waterdown, Waterford, Waterloo, Welland, Wellesley, West Flamborough, Westport, Whitby, Windsor, Wingham, Woodstock, York, Zorra

Book 238-239: Ingersoll
Book 240: Zorra Township
Book 241: Southwest Oxford
Book 242:Otterville,Burgessville

The Township of Norwich is located in Oxford County in southwestern Ontario. Pioneering families emigrated from Norwich in upper New York State in the early 19th century. Oxford County Road 59 is the major north-south highway through much of the township, including the community of Norwich proper. The local economy is largely agricultural, based on corn, soybean, and wheat production with dairy farming in the north part of the township and tobacco, vegetable, and ginseng farming to the south. Slowly, ginseng and traditional cash crops are replacing the former cash crop - tobacco, as demand shrinks.

In 1799, the Township of Norwich was laid out by surveyor William Hambly into lines and concessions and 200-acre lots. The township was divided into North and South Norwich Townships in 1855.

In 1975, Oxford County underwent countywide municipal restructuring. The Village of Norwich and the Townships of East Oxford, North Norwich and South Norwich were amalgamated to create the Township of Norwich.

Norwich includes the communities of Beaconsfield, Bond's Corners, Brown's Corners, Burgessville, Cornell, Creditville, Curries, Eastwood, Hawtrey, Hink's Corners, Holbrook, Milldale, Muir, Newark, New Durham, Norwich, Oriel, Otterville, Oxford Centre, Rock's Mills, Rosanna, Springford, Summerville, Blows, and Vandecar.

Otterville is a village in Norwich Township in Oxford County. It is located on the Otter Creek. Otterville was settled in 1807. Encouraged by local Quakers, free blacks and escaped slaves fled persecution in the United States and found homes in the Otterville area beginning in 1829. Otterville African Methodist Episcopal Church and Cemetery served the local black community until the late 1880s.

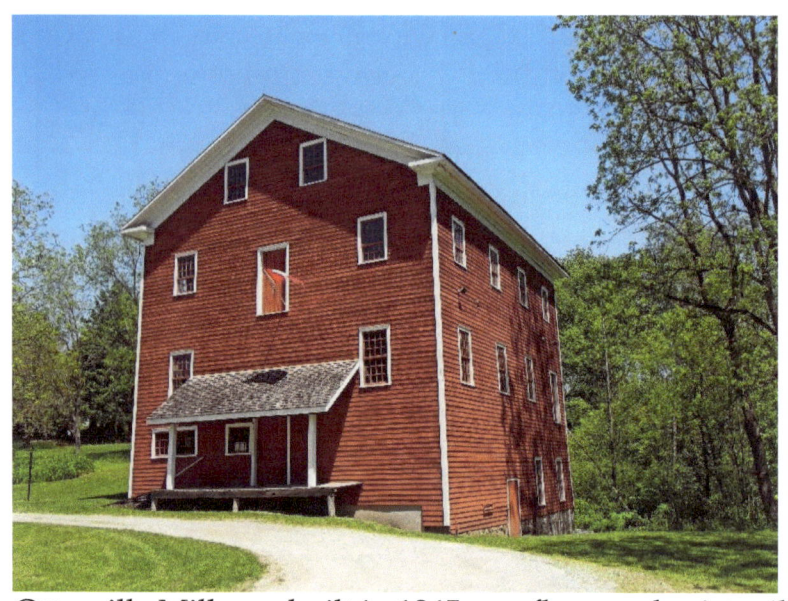

The Otterville Mill was built in 1845 as a flour and grist mill by Edward Bullock and operated by Matthew Maddison. It is located on the Otter River. The Bullocks had saw and woollen mills above the present dam.

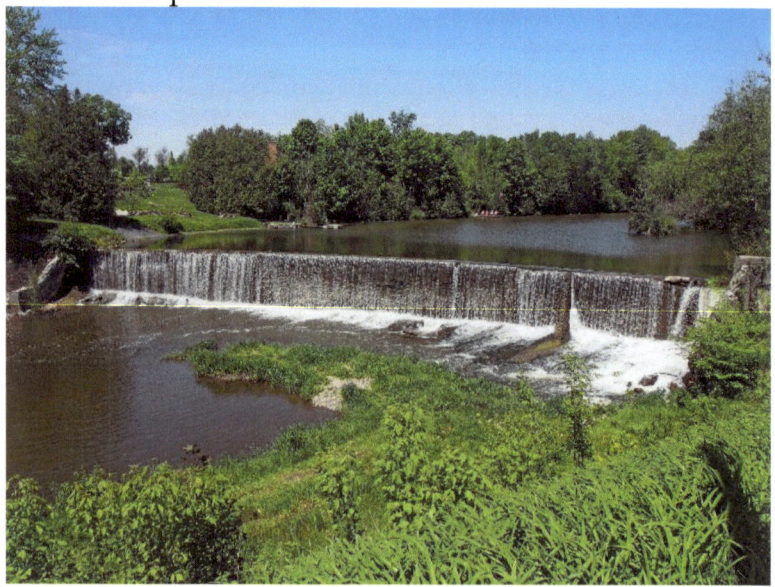

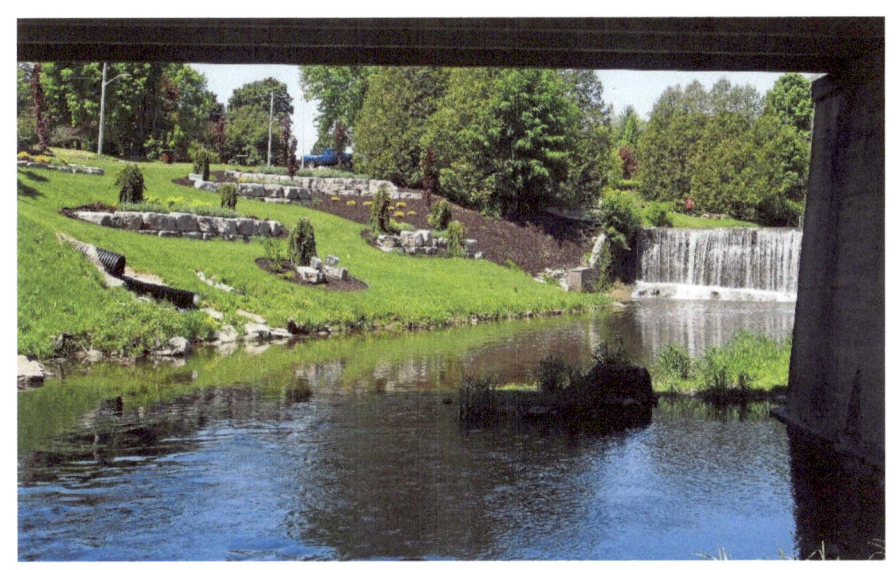

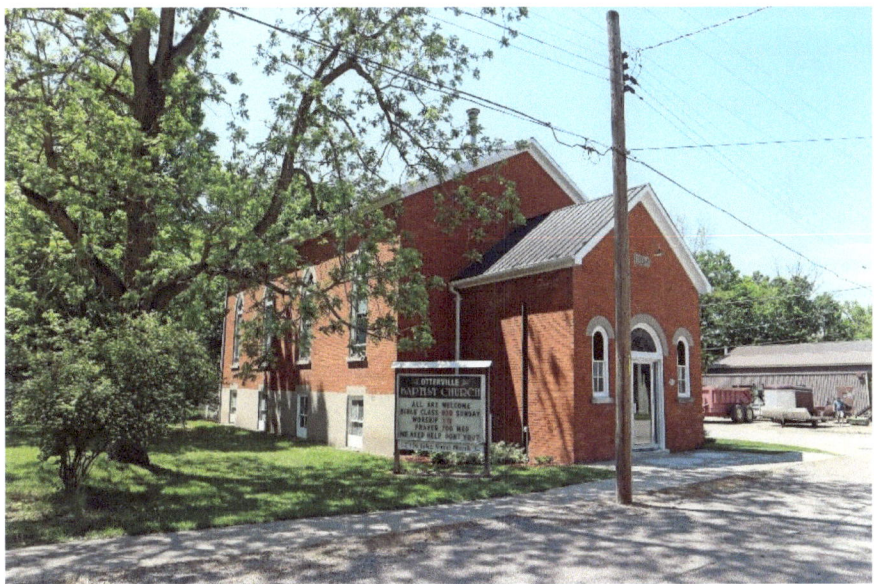

106 John Street North – Otterville Baptist Church – built in 1904

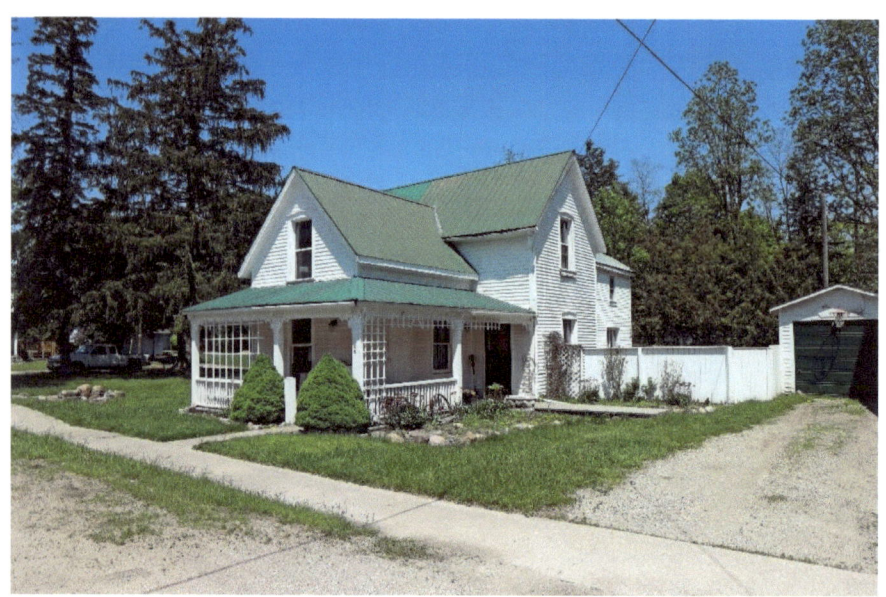

108 John Street - Gothic

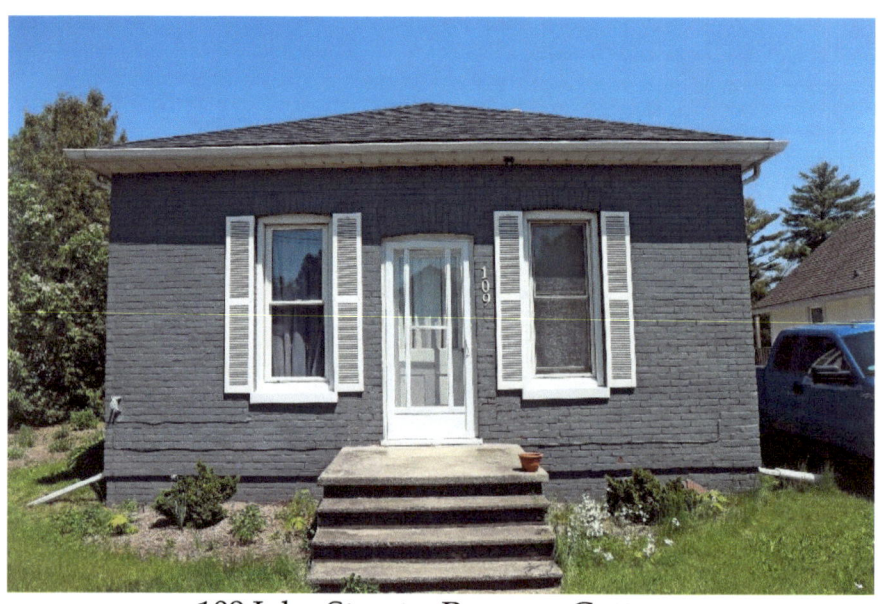

109 John Street – Regency Cottage

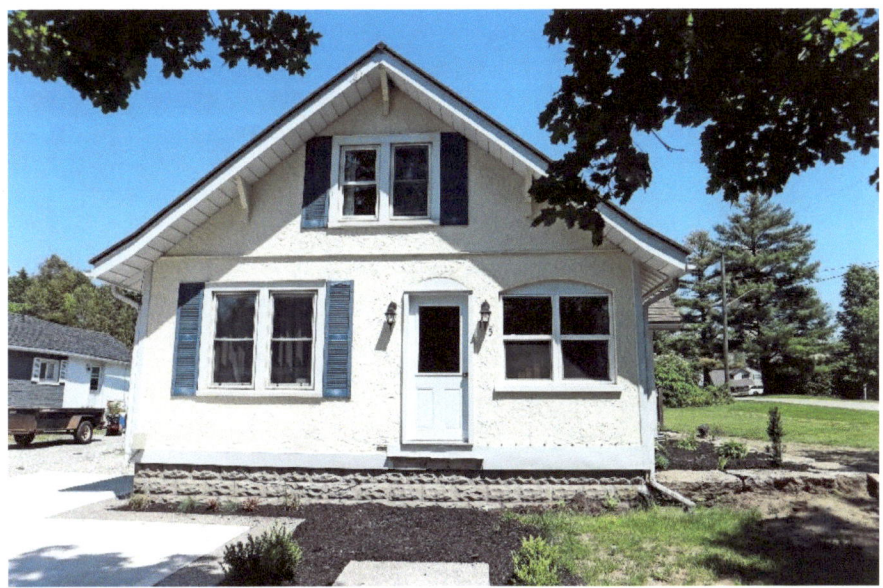

115 John Street

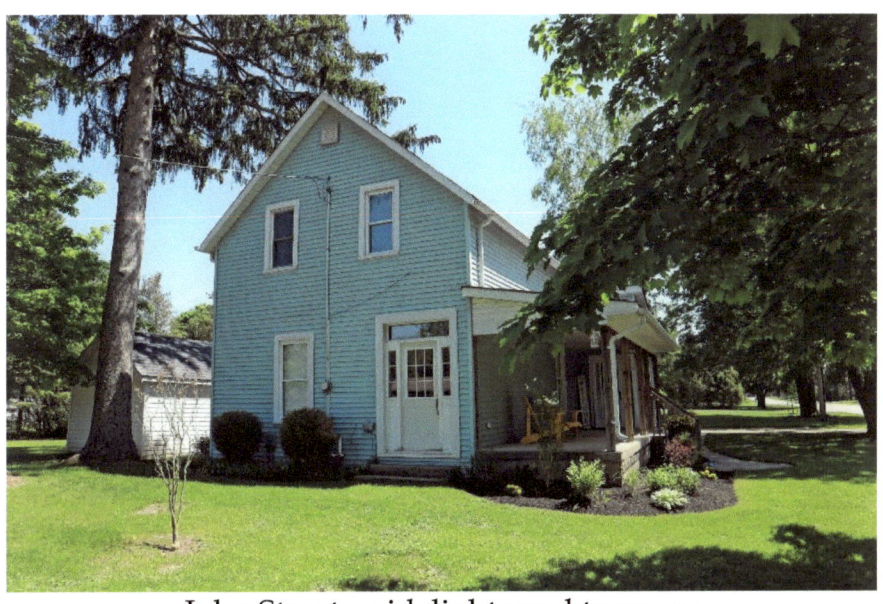

John Street – sidelights and transom

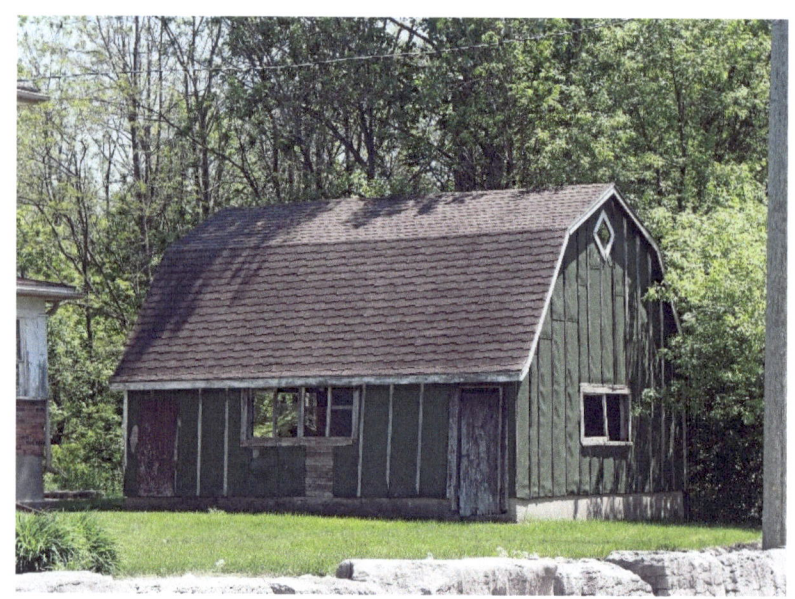
Gambrel roof

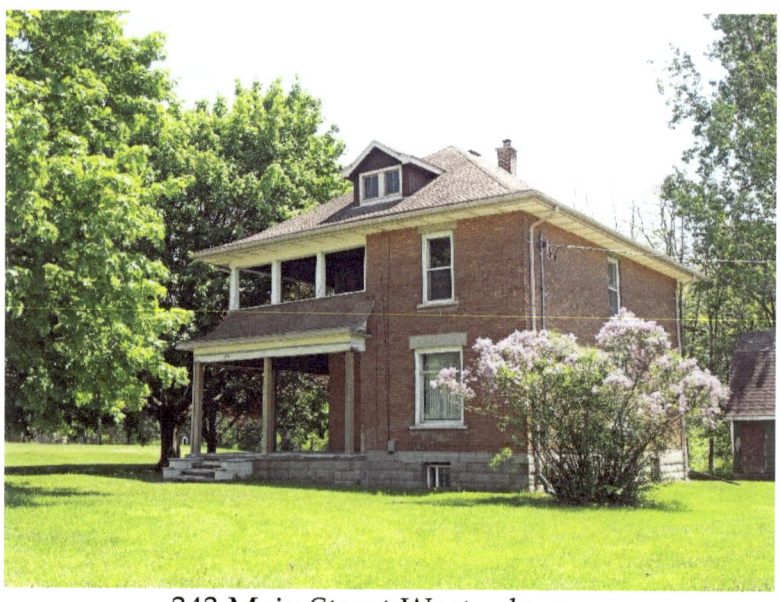
343 Main Street West - dormer

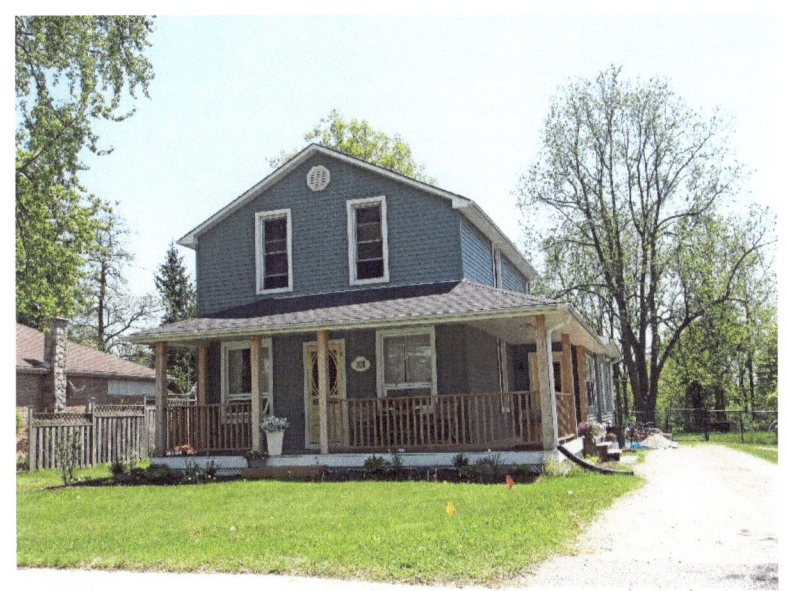

331 Main Street West

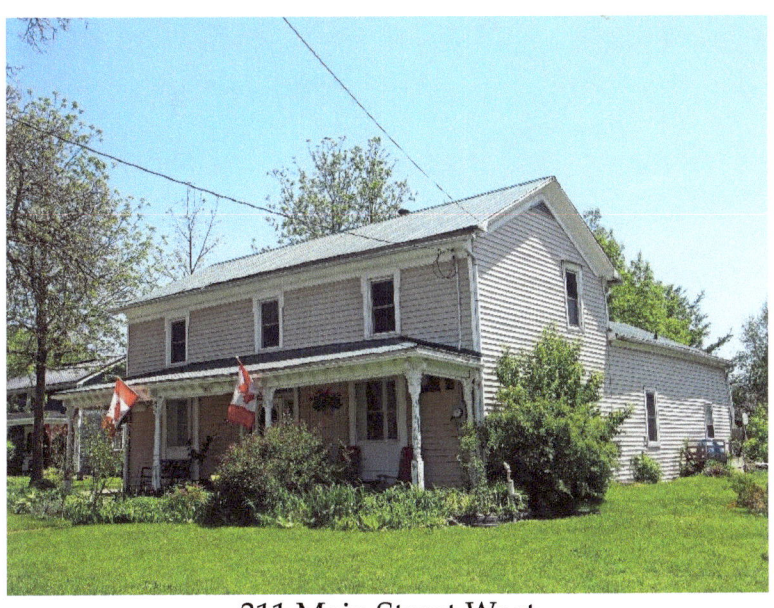

311 Main Street West

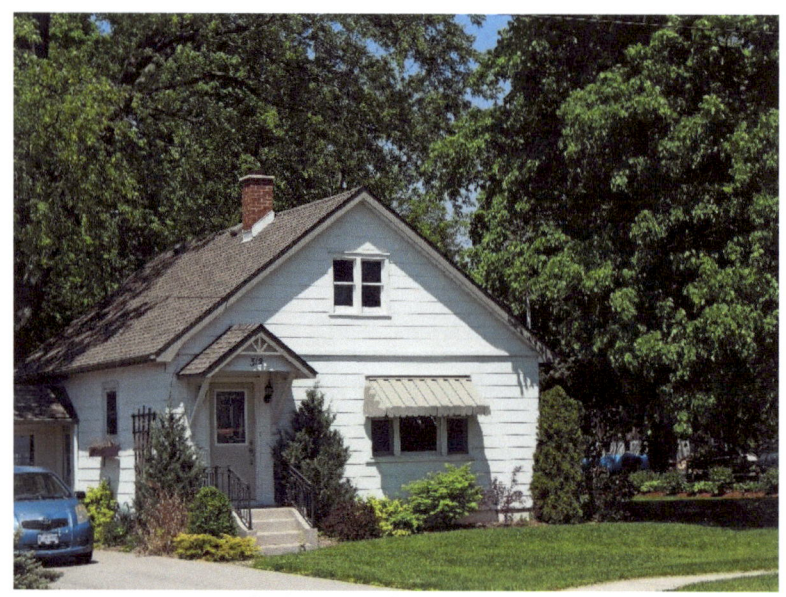

312 Main Street West

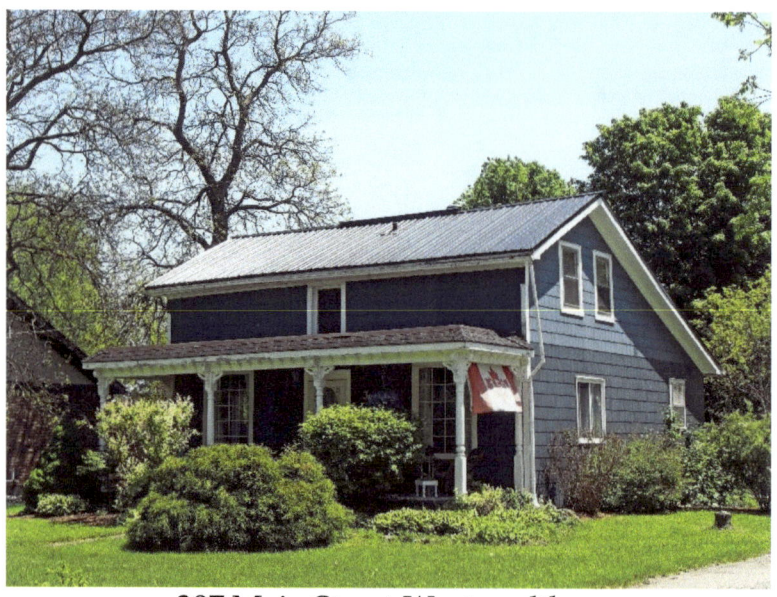

307 Main Street West - saltbox

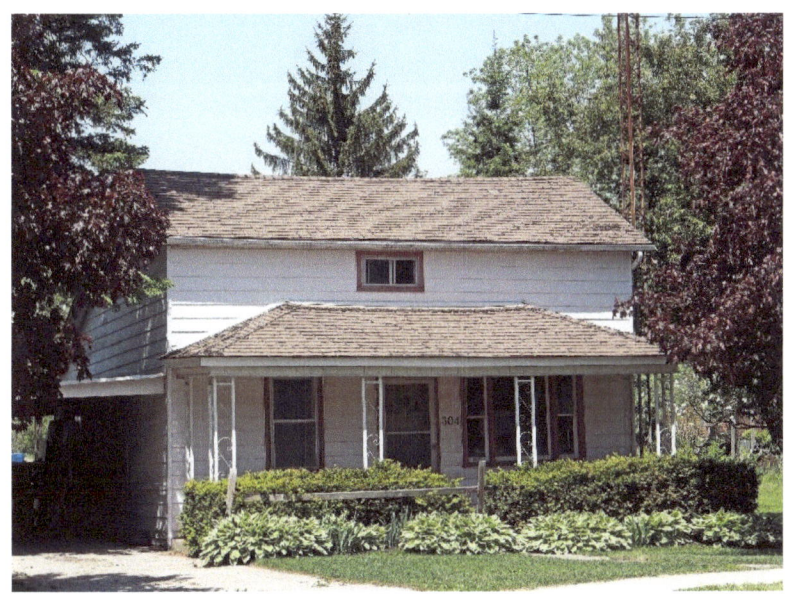

304 Main Street West

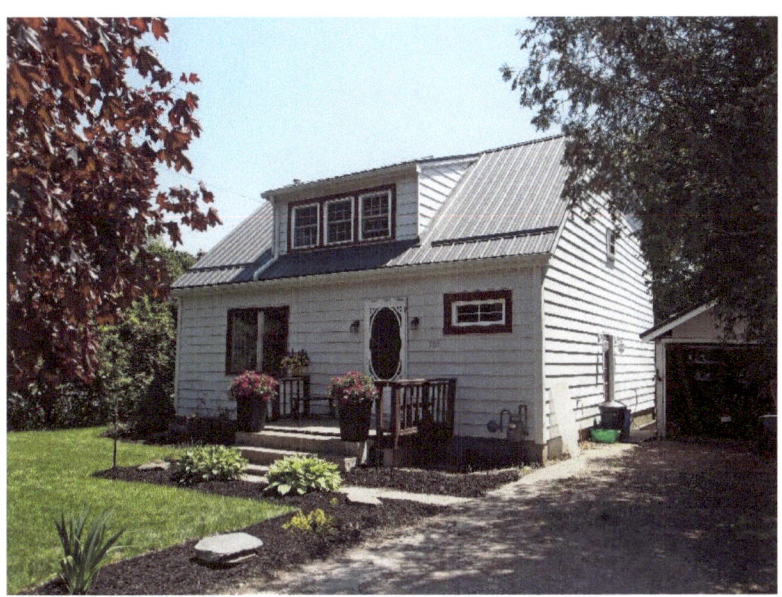

301 Main Street West – shed dormer

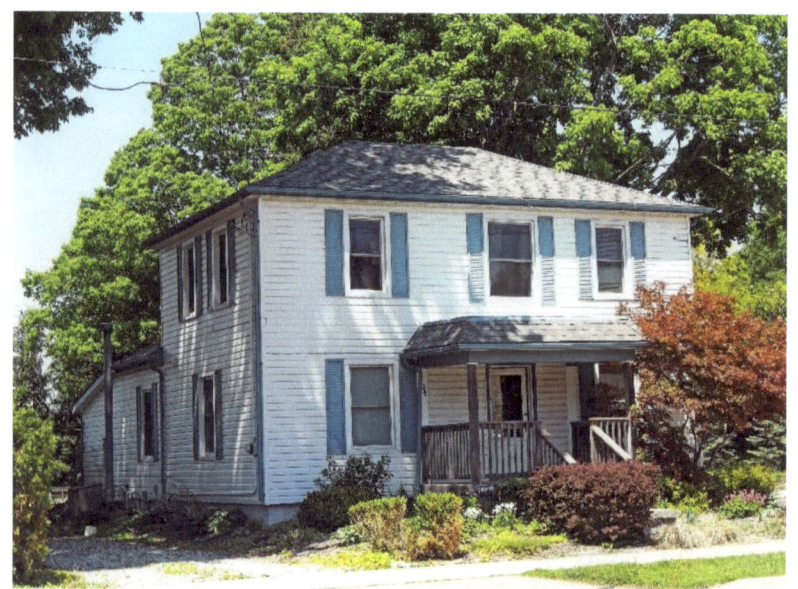
294 Main Street West – hipped roof

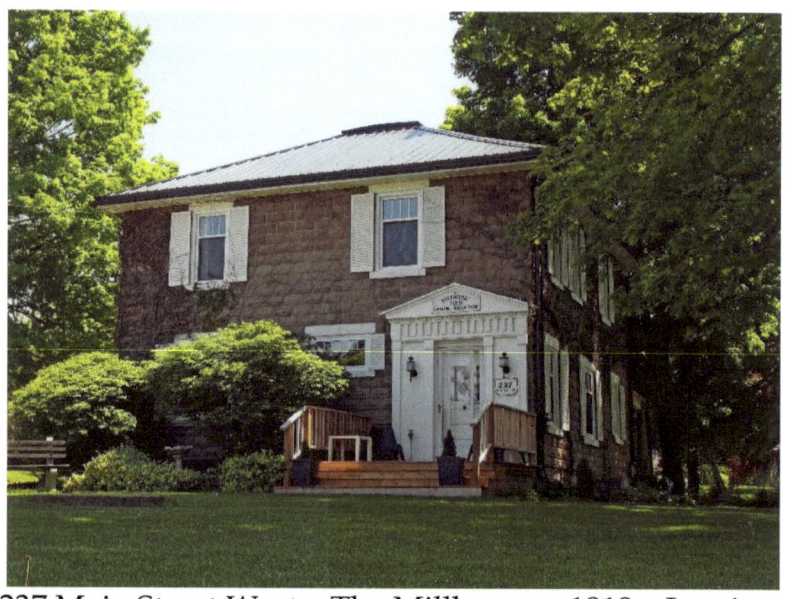
237 Main Street West – The Millhouse – 1919 – Lossing-Mountain

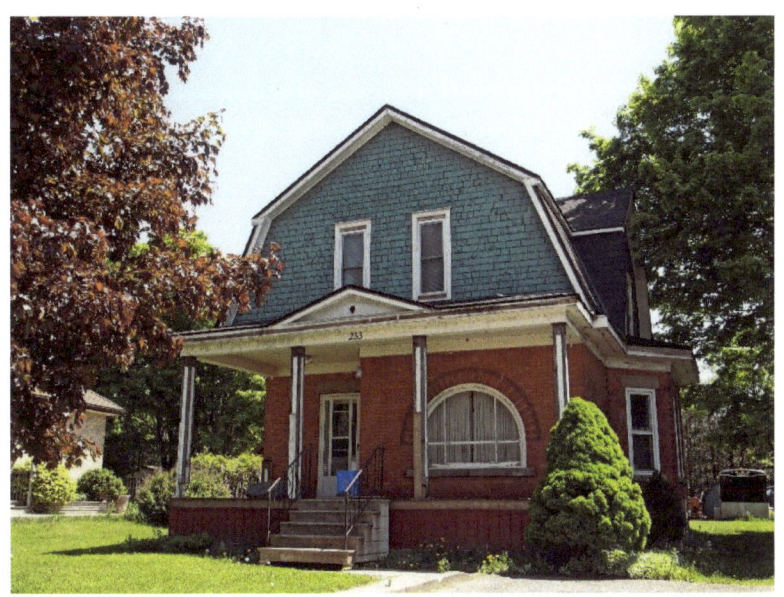

233 Main Street West – Neo-Colonial – gambrel roof, Romanesque-style window voussoirs

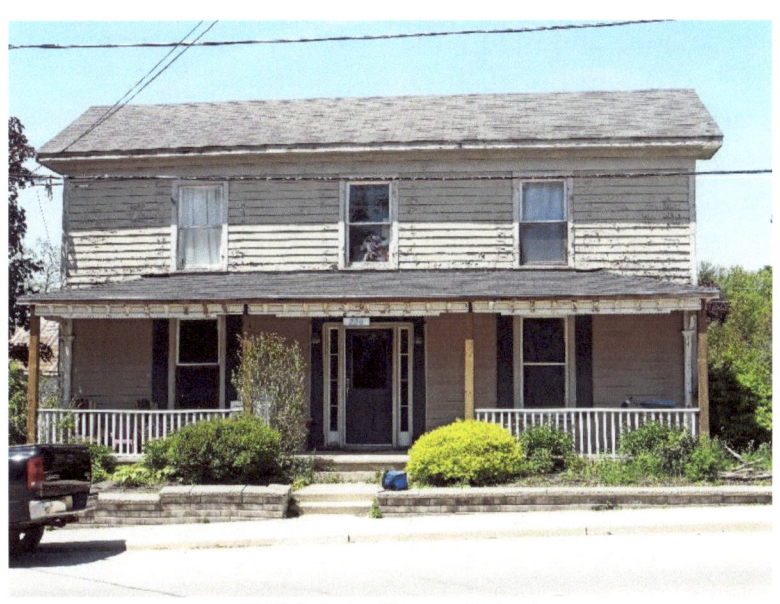

230 Main Street West

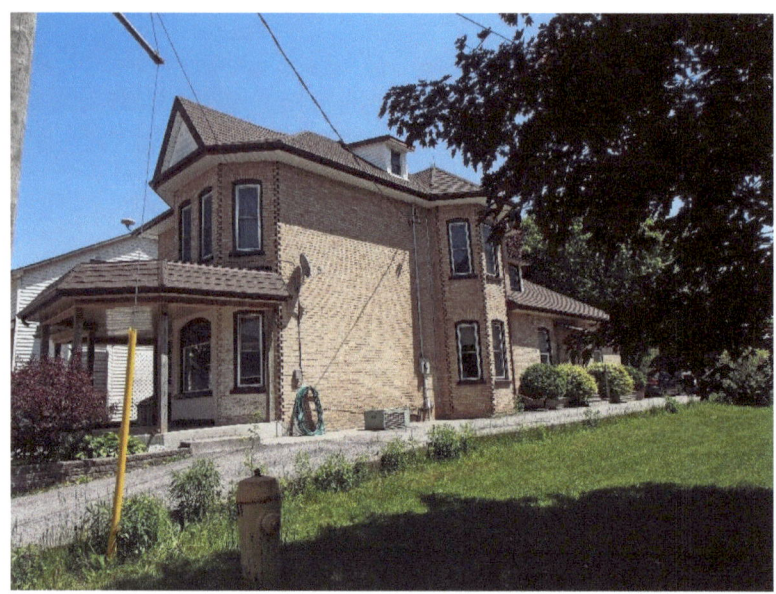

Main Street West – Lianne Todd Gallery and Studio

Lianne Todd is a watercolour and digital artist living in Otterville, Ontario. Lianne strives to capture a moment, a place or an idea and to lure the viewer in. Her watercolours vary between traditional and non-traditional, both in application and in subject matter. They are usually vivid reflections of nature and its patterns. Her paintings reflect her attachment to the land, her interest in science, her childhood on the farm, summers on lakes in northern Ontario, hikes through the woods, crisp winter days, flowers in the garden, music, pets, and her two children. They are images of the places, people, and patterns of nature that she loves.

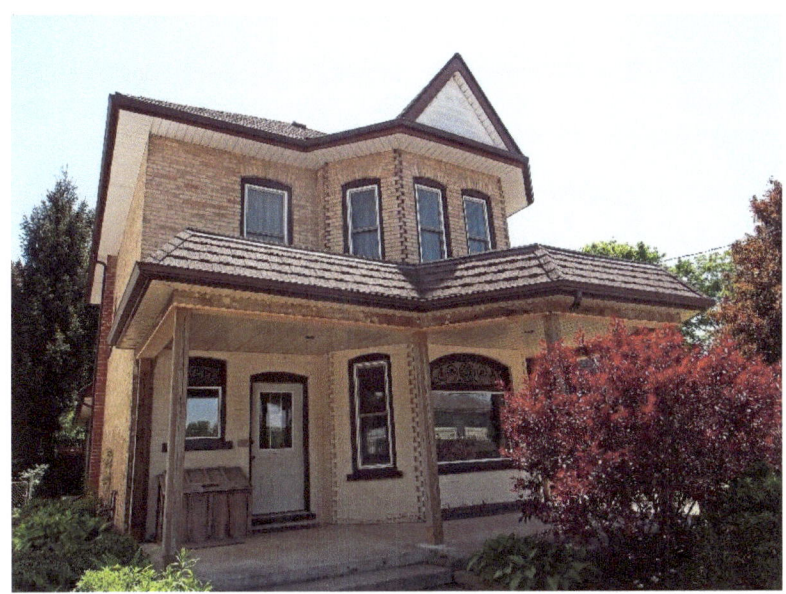

Main Street West – stained glass transoms

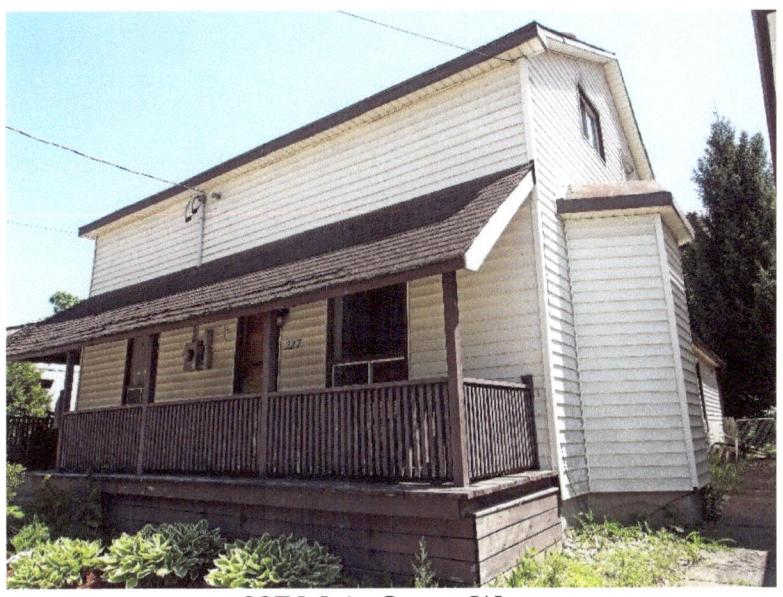

227 Main Street West

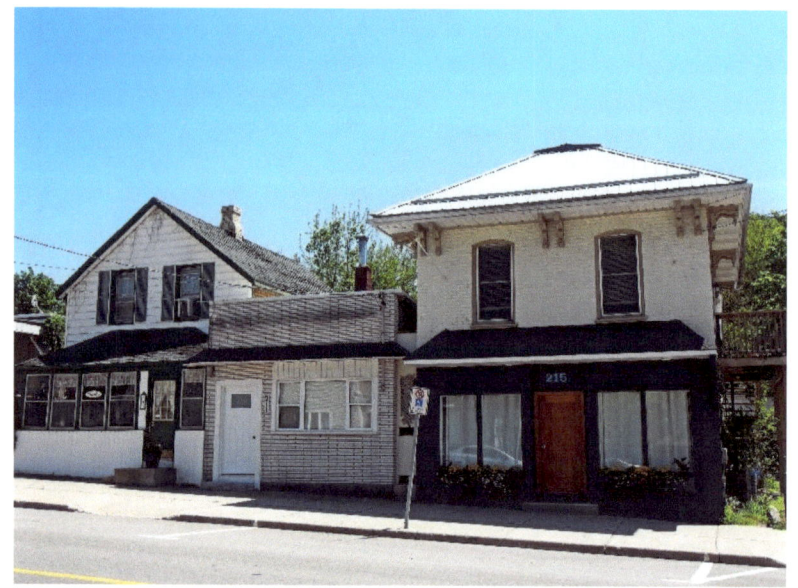

209-215 Main Street West – cornice brackets, hipped roof

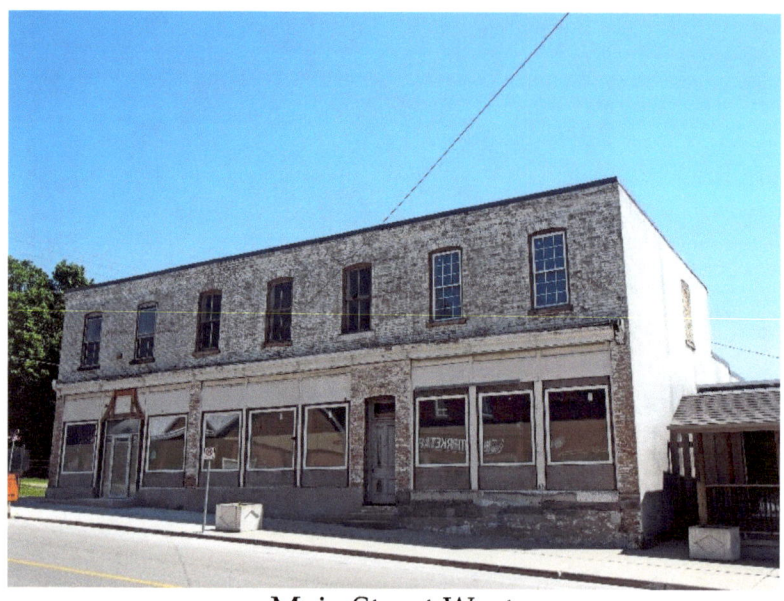

Main Street West

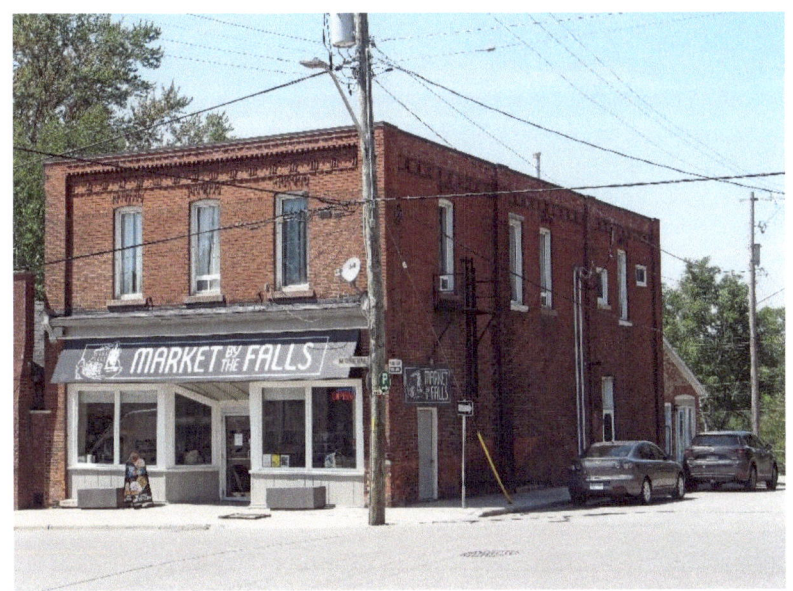

202 Main Street West – Market by the Falls – dentil molding

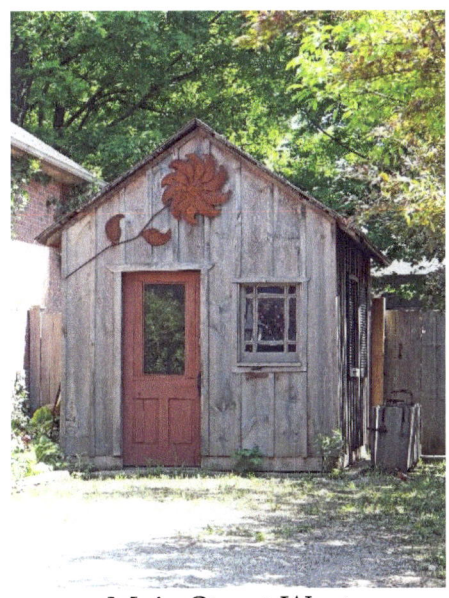

Main Street West

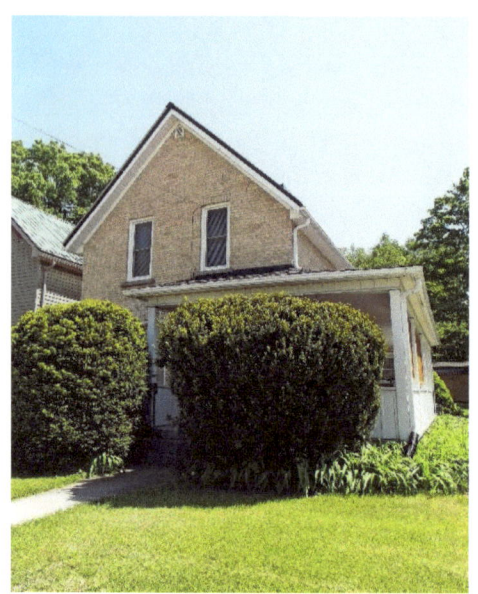

Main Street

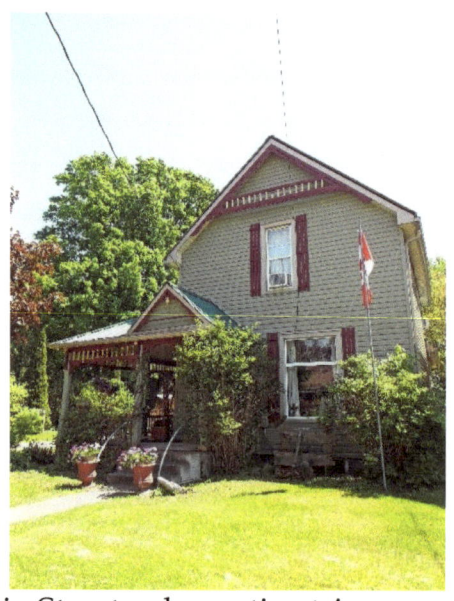

Main Street – decorative trim on gable

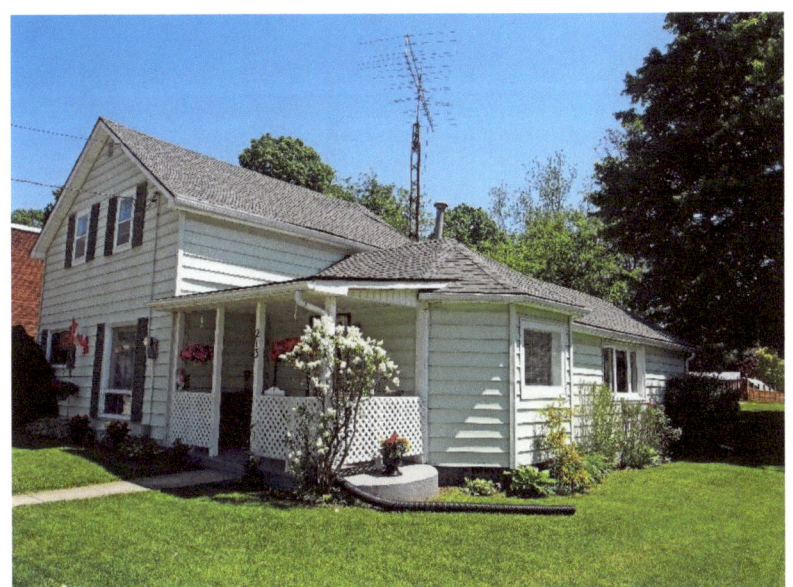

213 Main Street

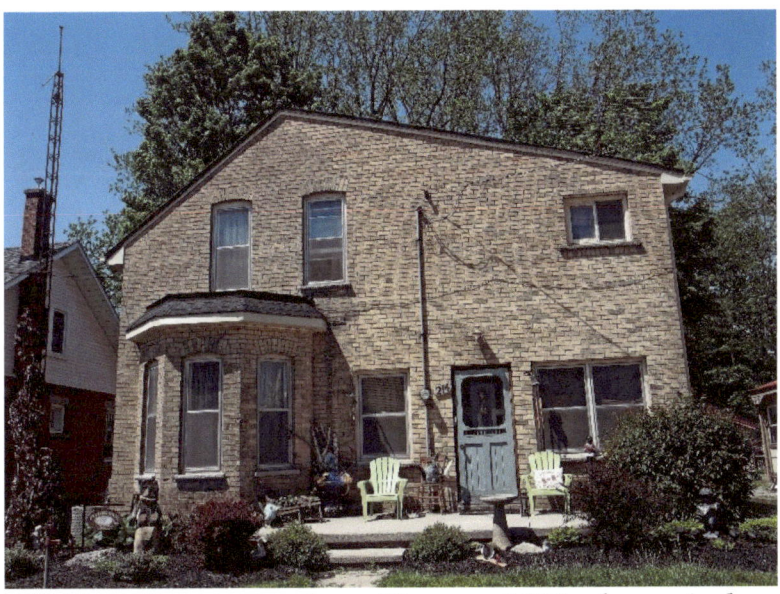

214 Main Street – Furlong House – 1889 – bay window

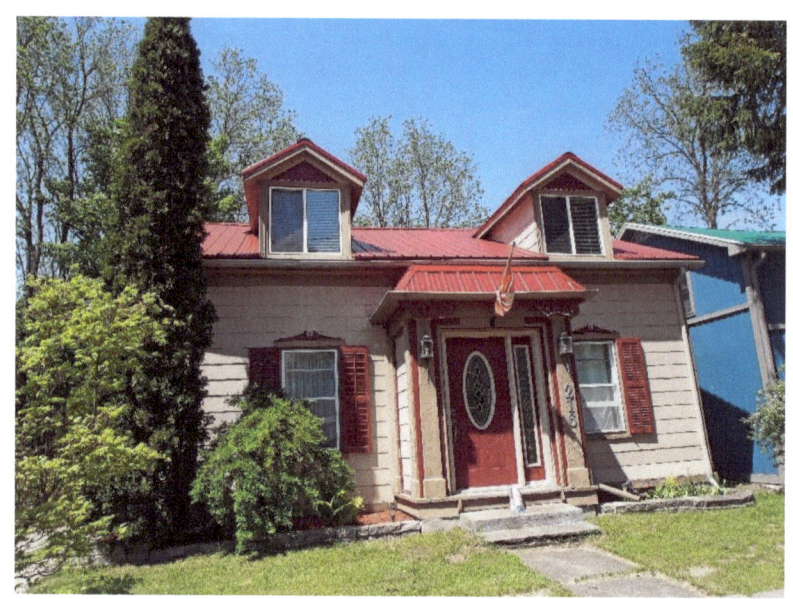
216 Main Street – dormers, sidelight

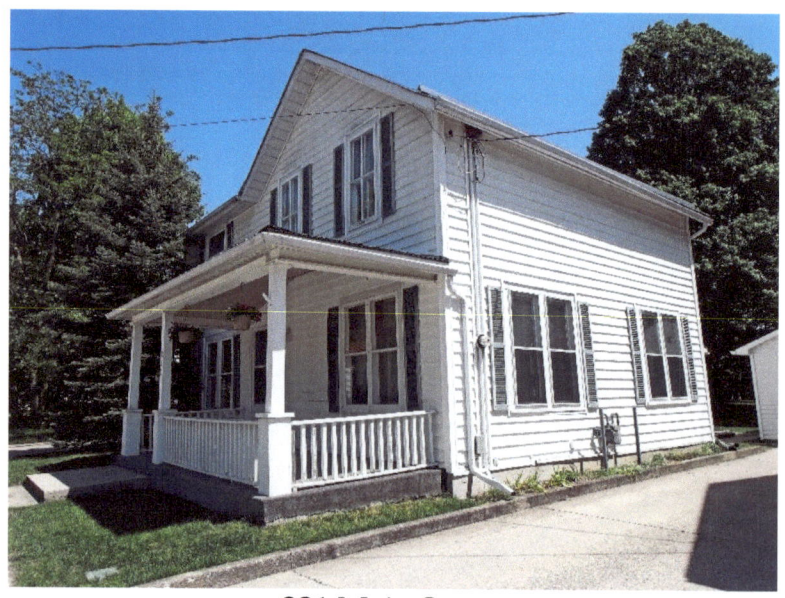
221 Main Street

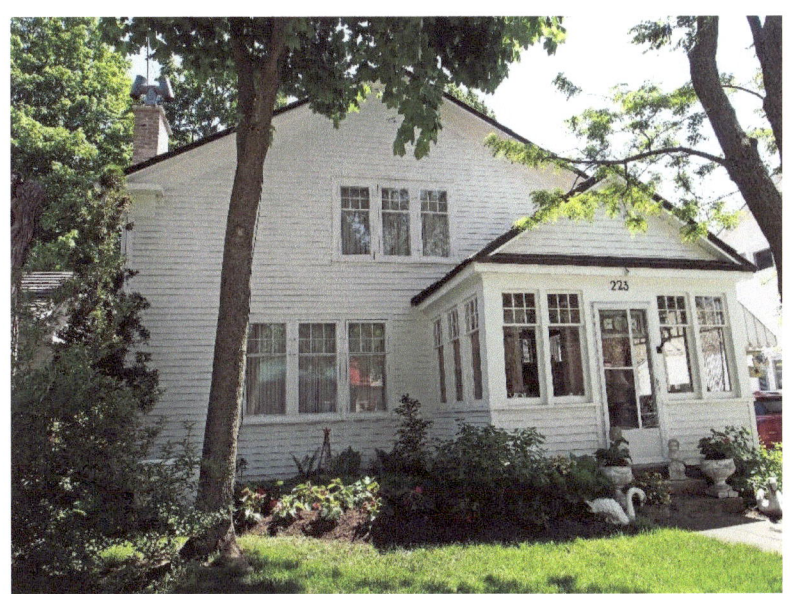

223 Main Street – enclosed front porch

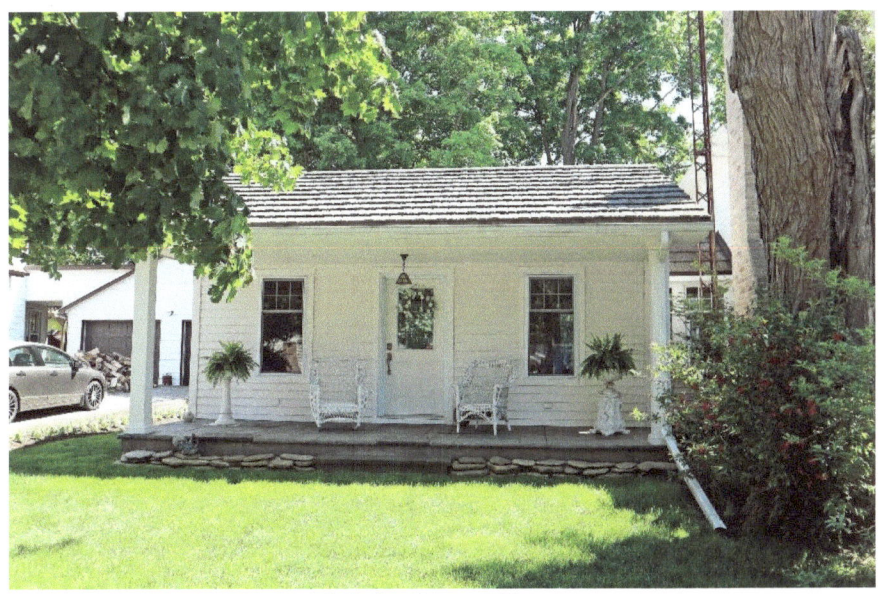

Main Street East

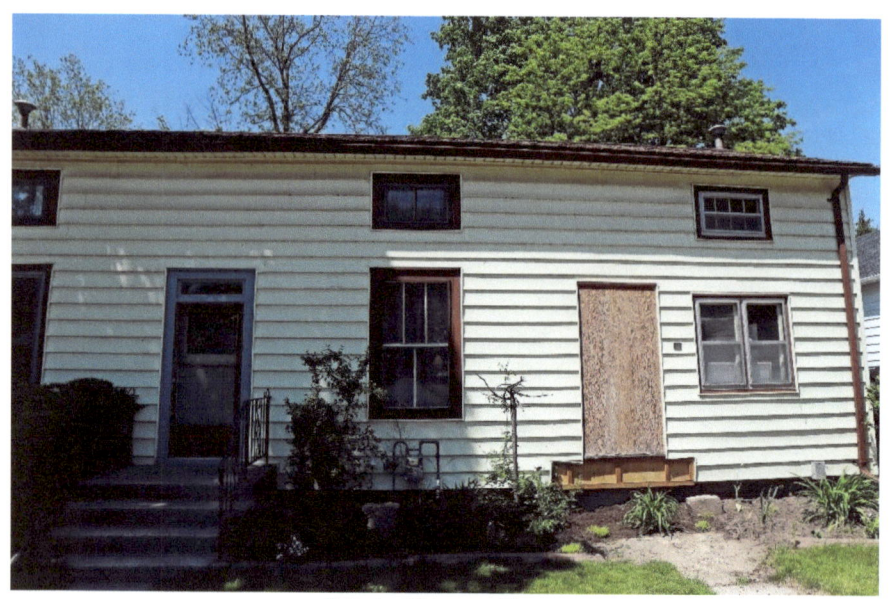
Main Street East

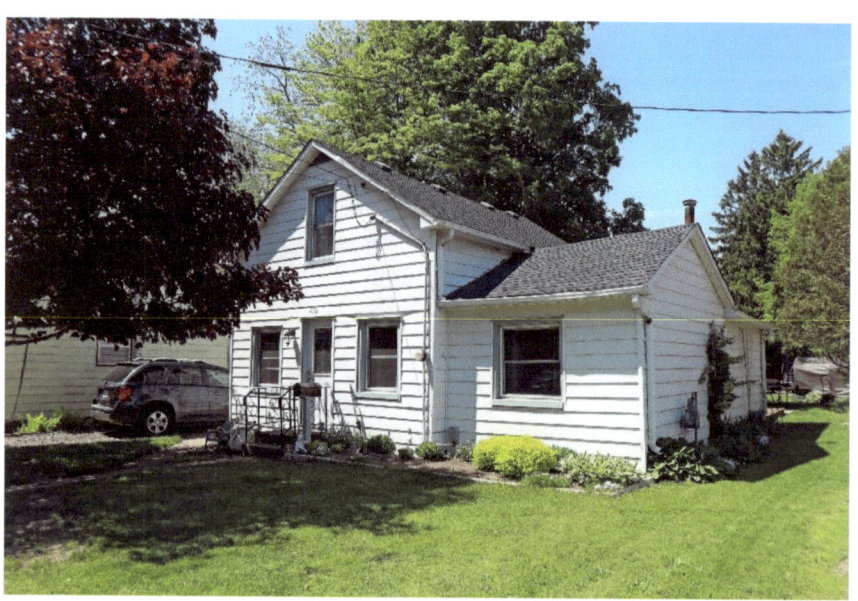
224 Main Street East

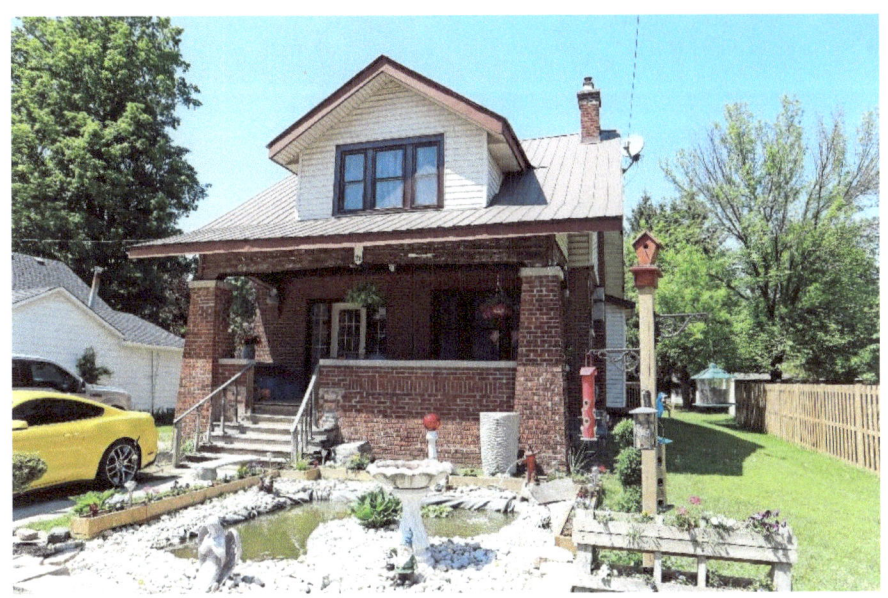

226 Main Street East – large dormer

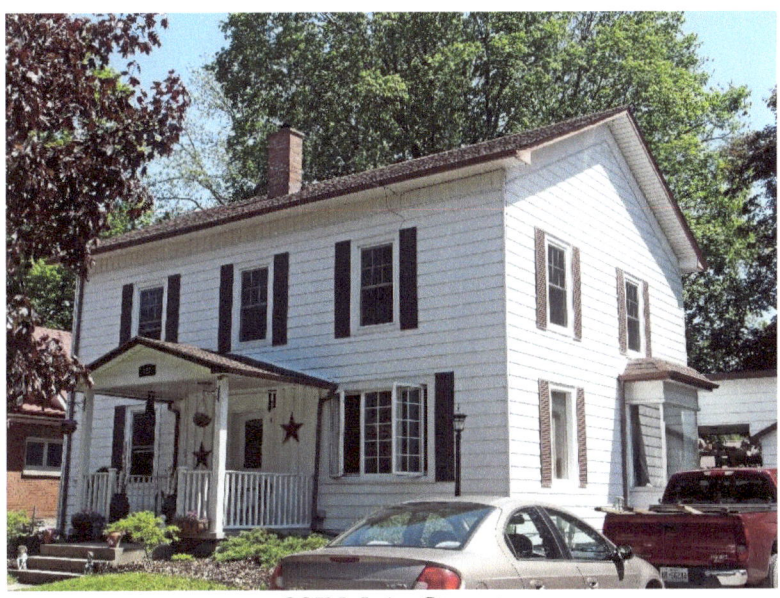

227 Main Street

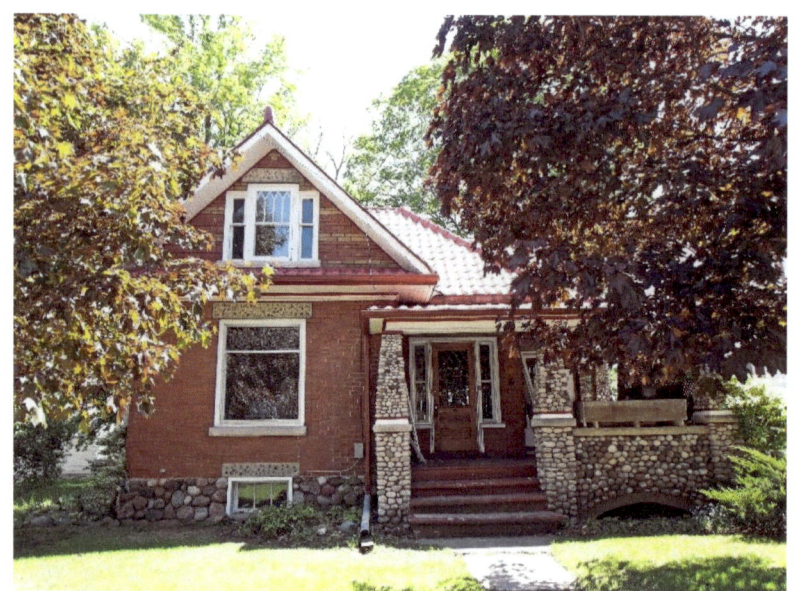

229 Main Street – Moore/Freeland House – cobblestone piers and veranda

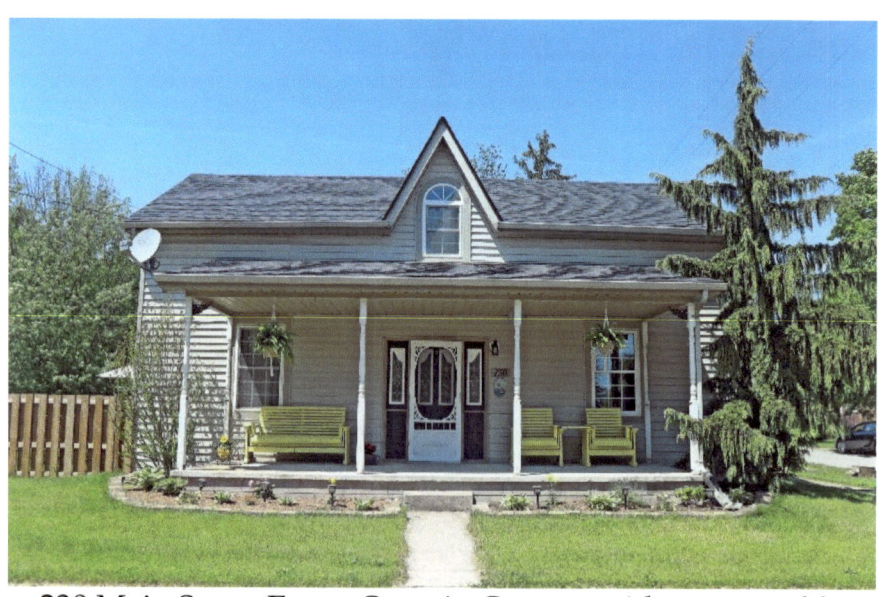

230 Main Street East – Ontario Cottage with centre gable

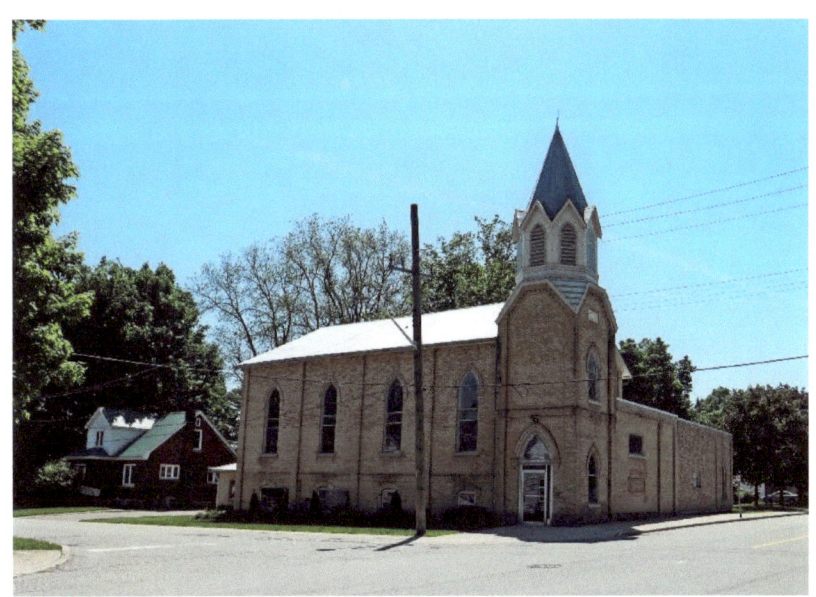

231 Main Street East – Otterville United Church – A.D. 1884 – Gothic Revival – lancet windows

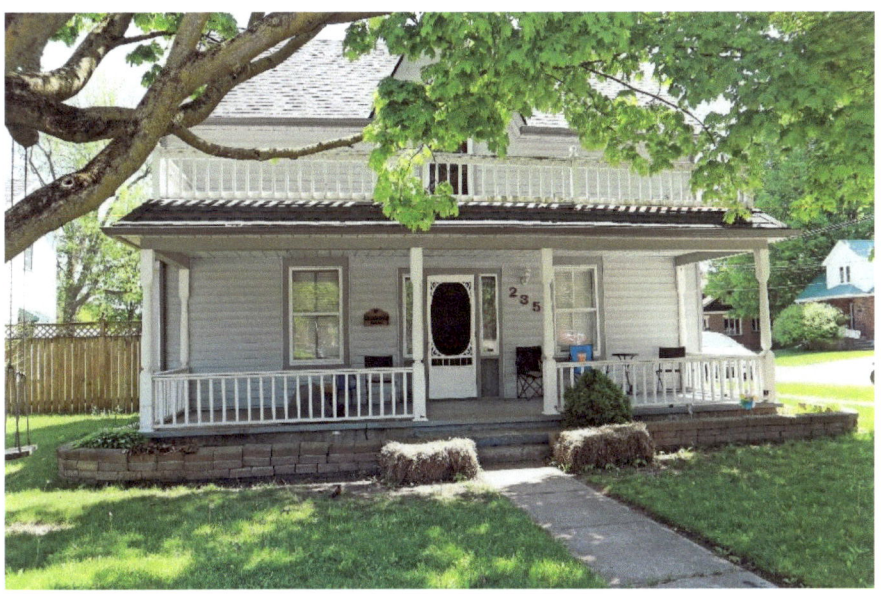

235 Main Street East – second-floor full-width balcony

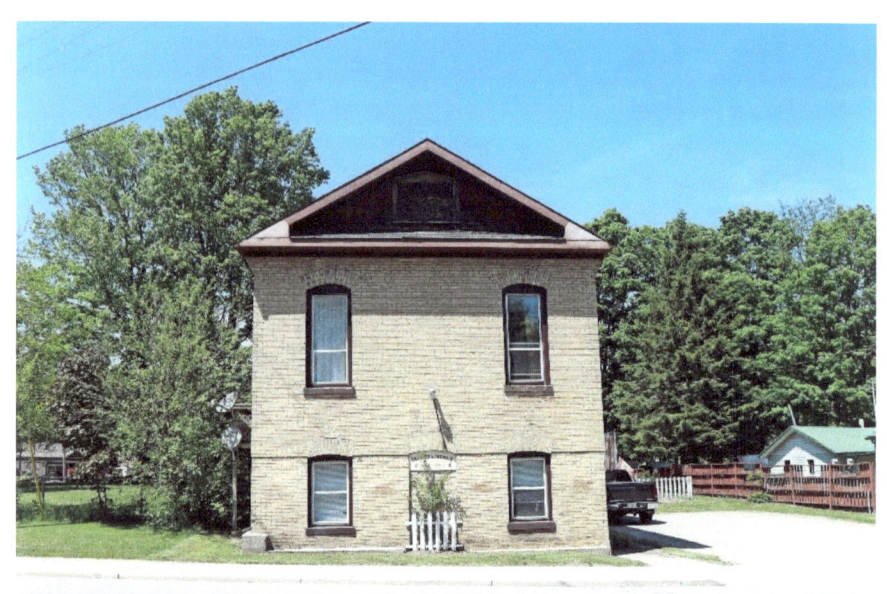
236 Main Street East

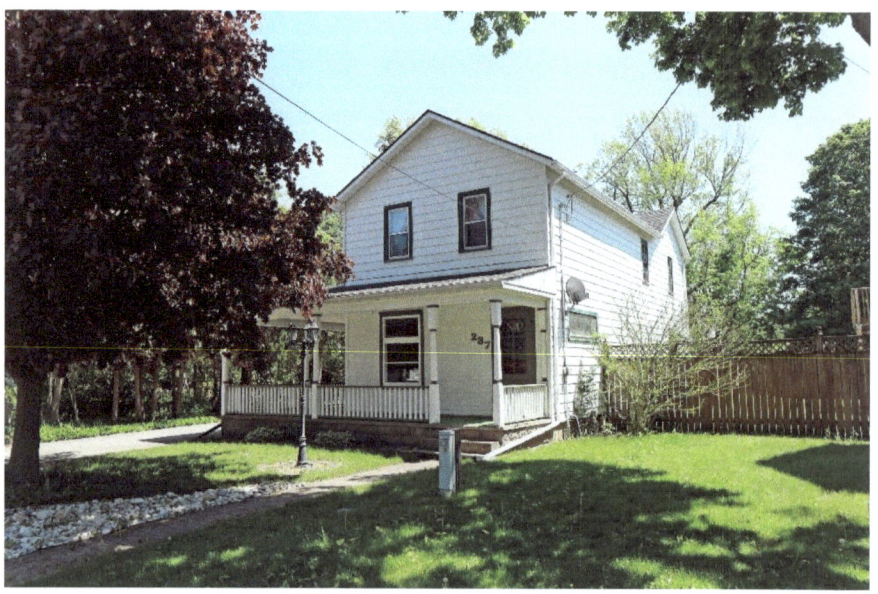
237 Main Street East

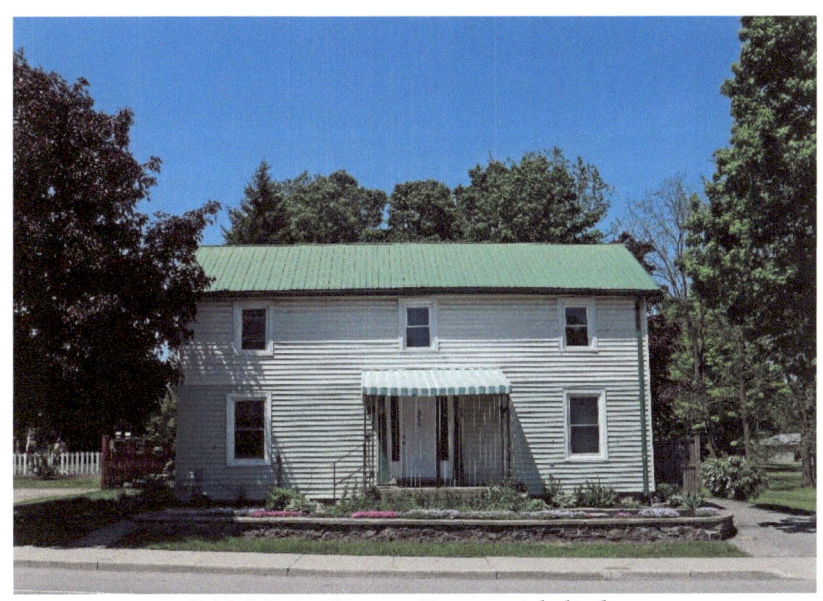

240 Main Street East - sidelights

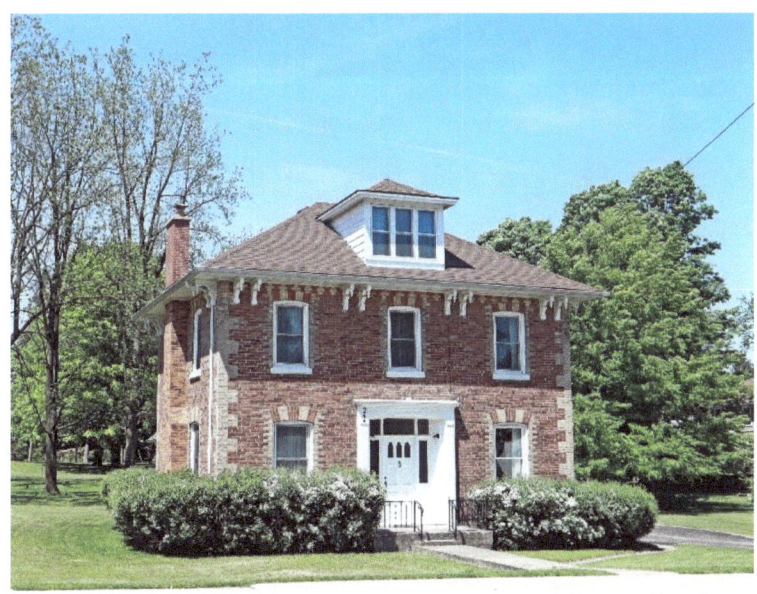

244 Main Street East – dormer in attic, paired cornice brackets, corner quoins, dichromatic voussoirs

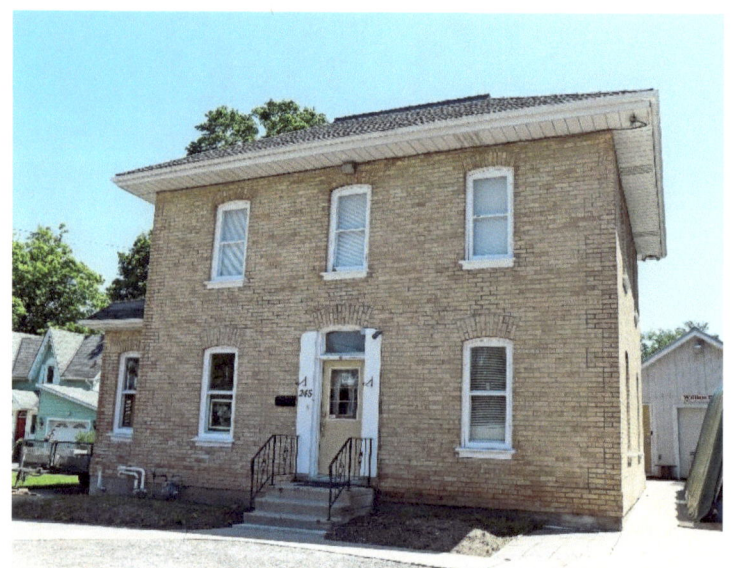

245 Main Street East – hipped roof, transom window above door

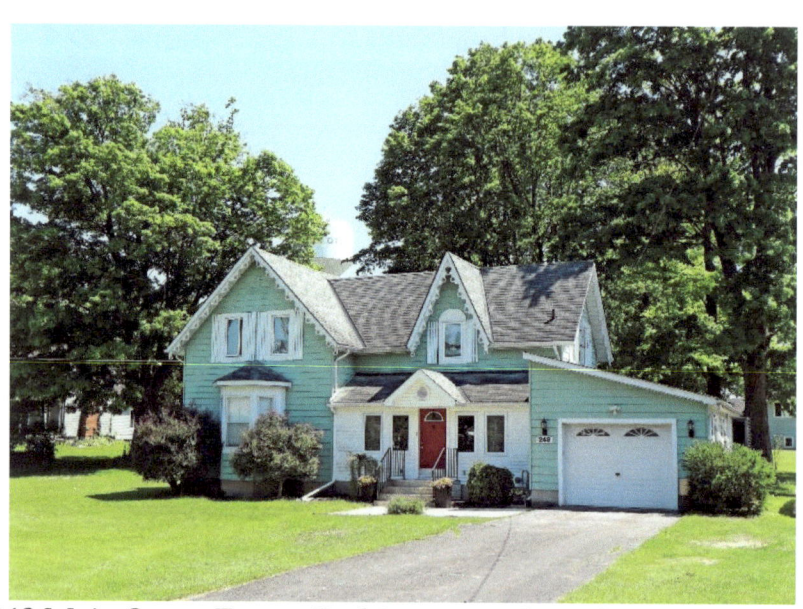

249 Main Street East – Gothic – verge board trim on gables

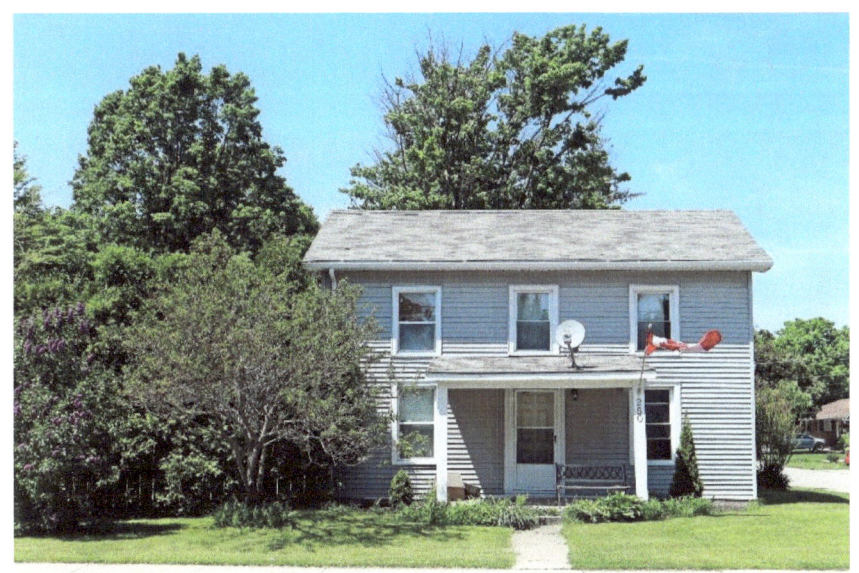

250 Main Street East

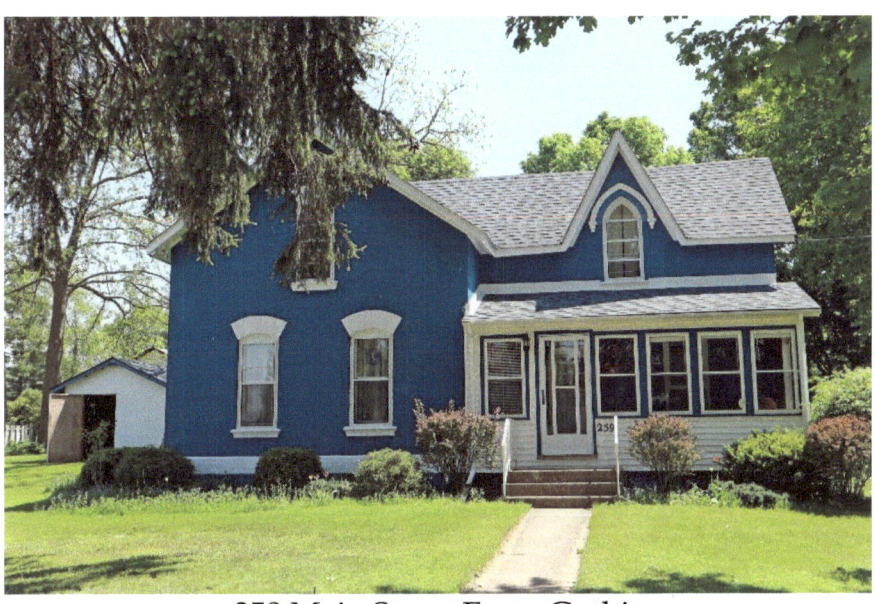

259 Main Street East - Gothic

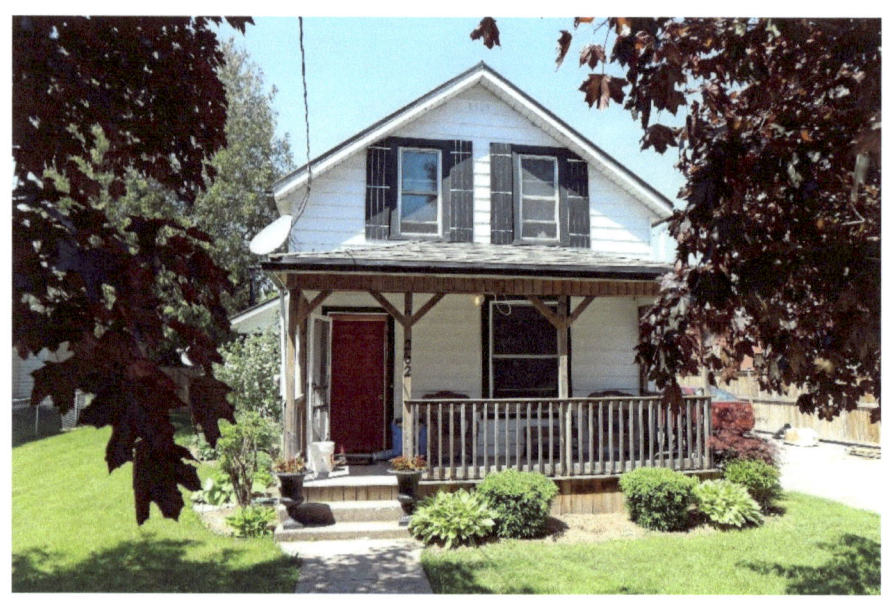

260 Main Street East

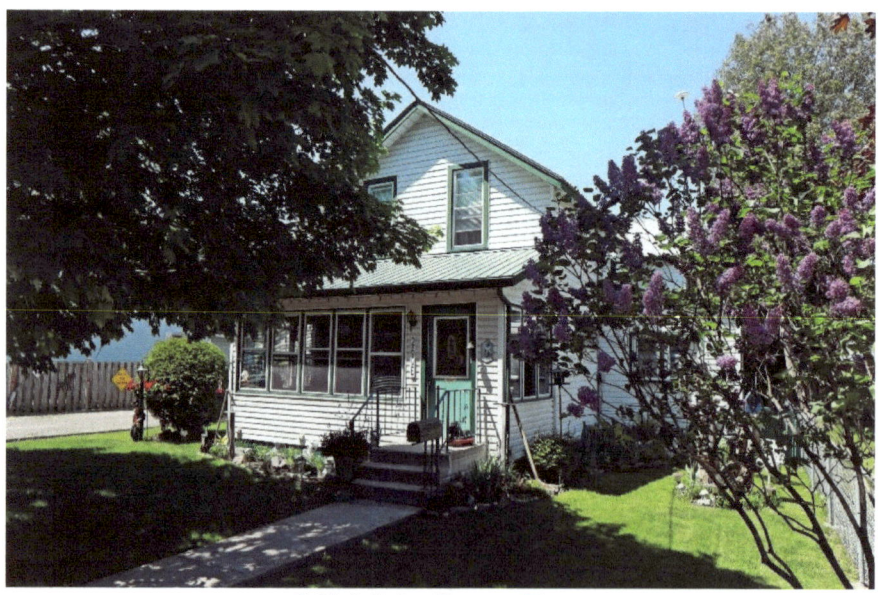

262 Main Street East

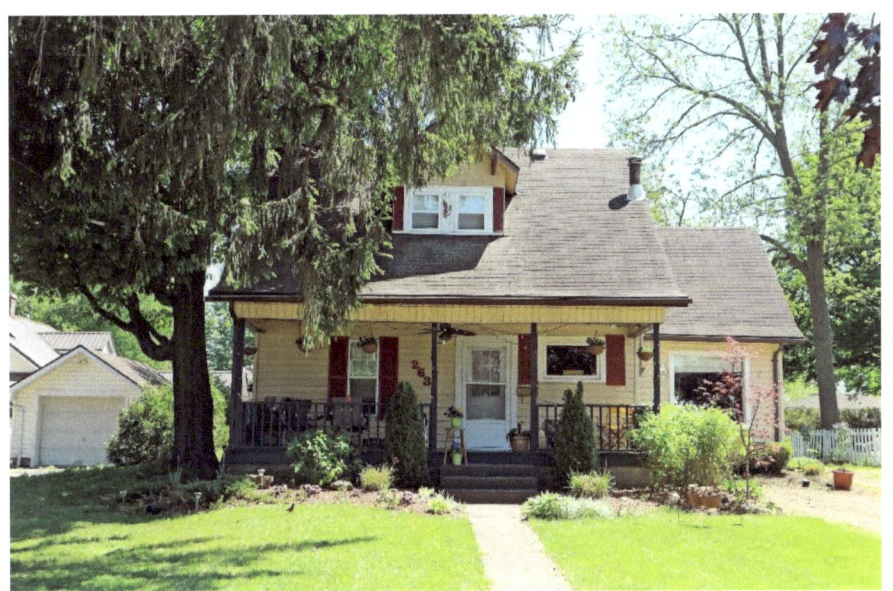

263 Main Street East - dormer

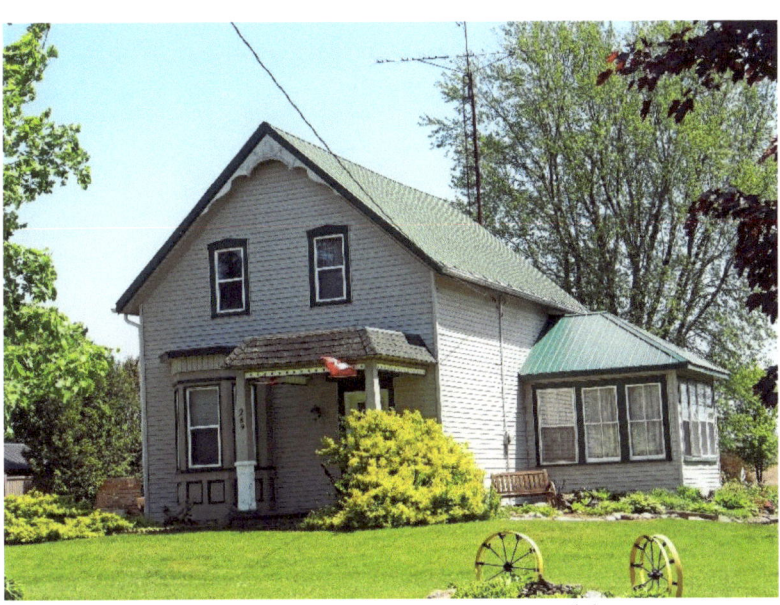

289 Main Street – trim on gable

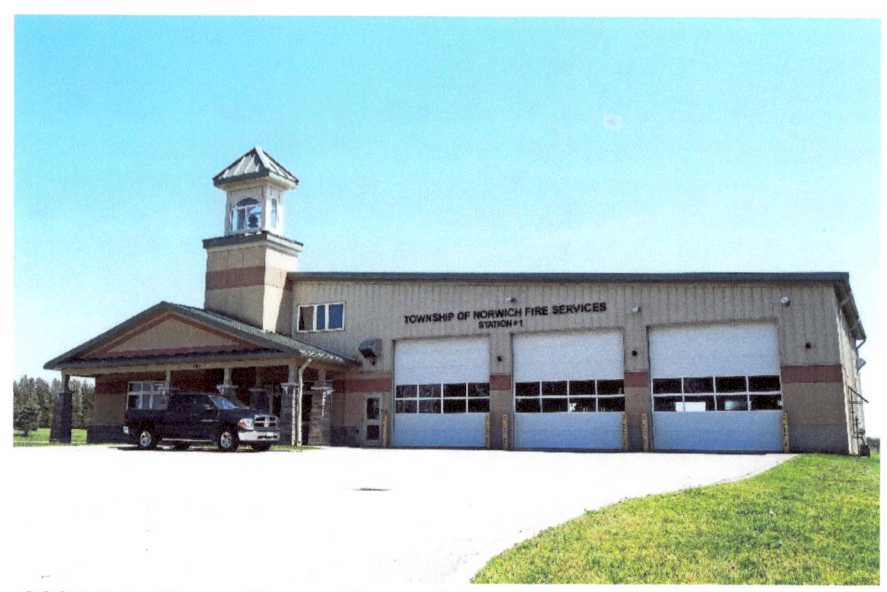

309 Main Street East – Township of Norwich Fire Station #1

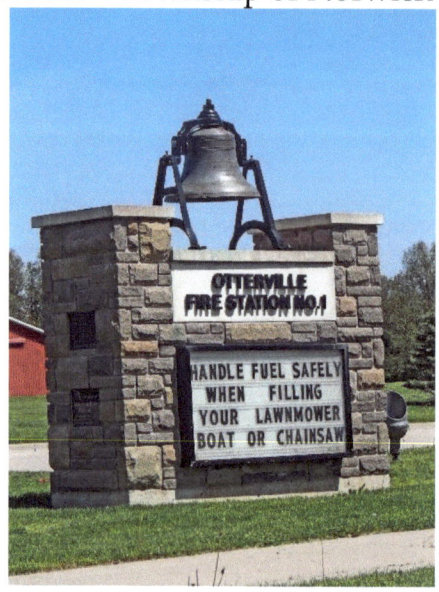

For over 60 years the old town bell that now rests silently on its stone foundation near the South Norwich Firehall rang out daily in the community life of the residents of Otterville. It was retired from use in 1941. The bell was cast in Troy, New York.

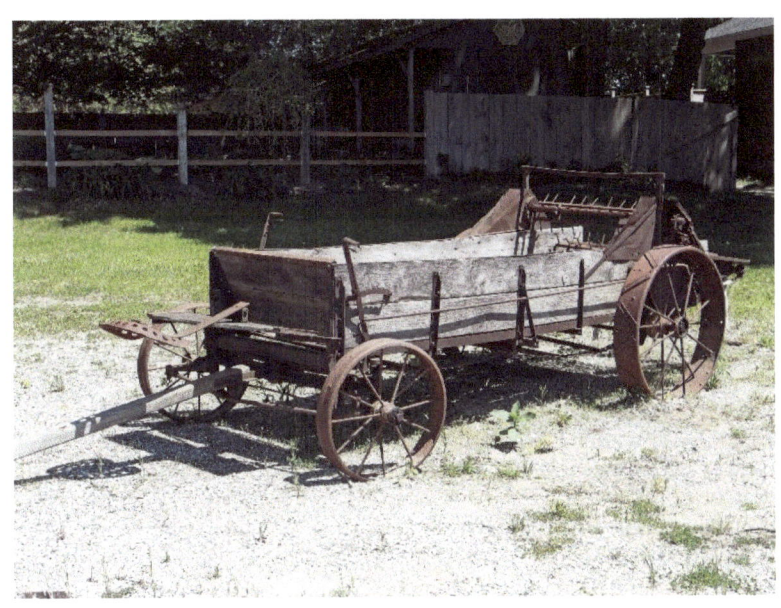

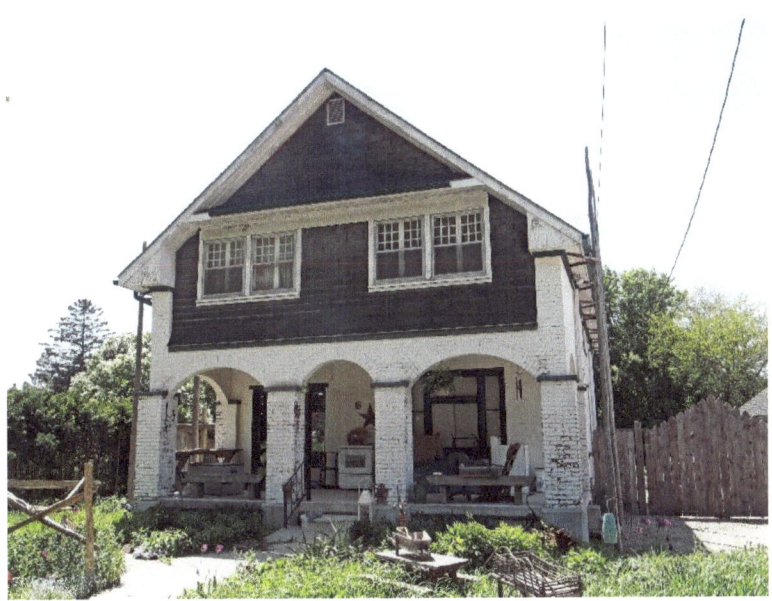

6 Dover Street

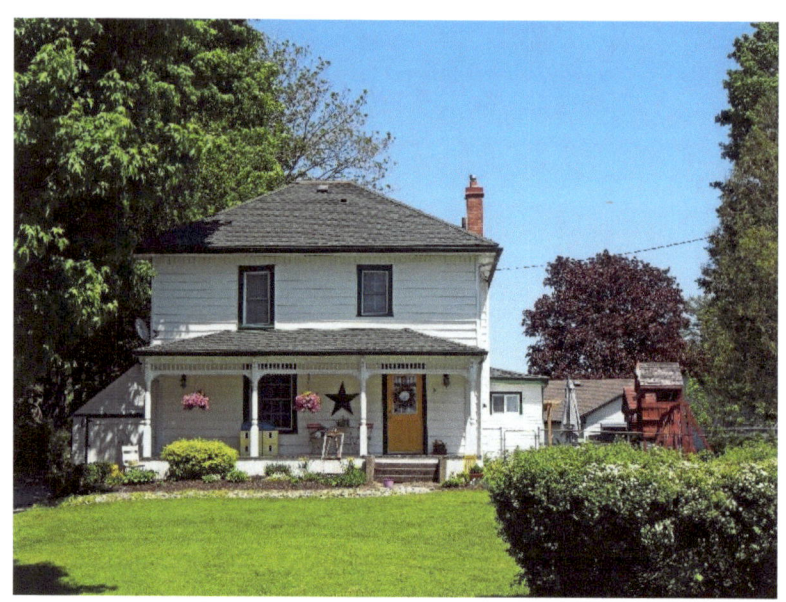

9 Dover Street – hipped roof

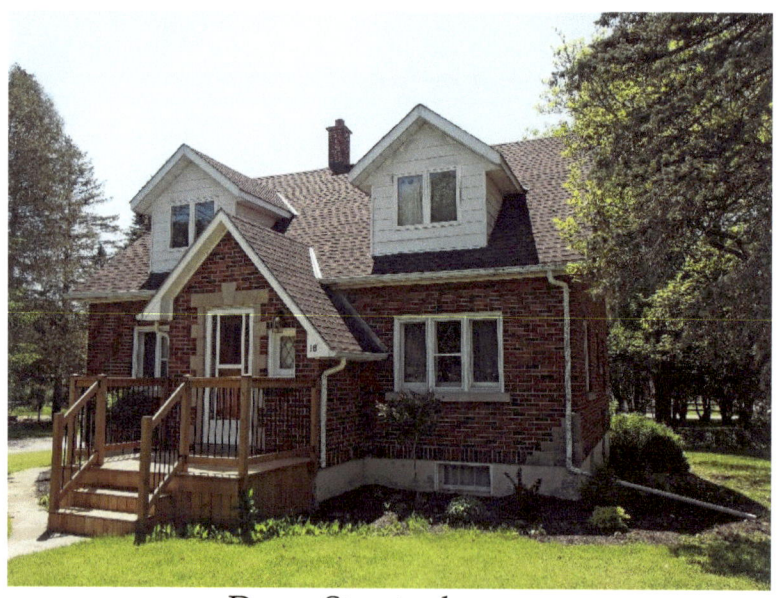

Dover Street - dormers

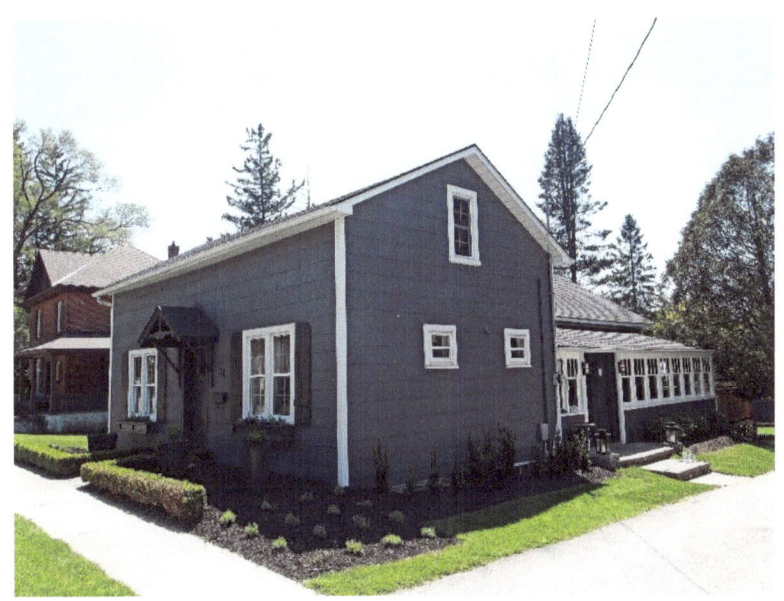

24 Dover Street

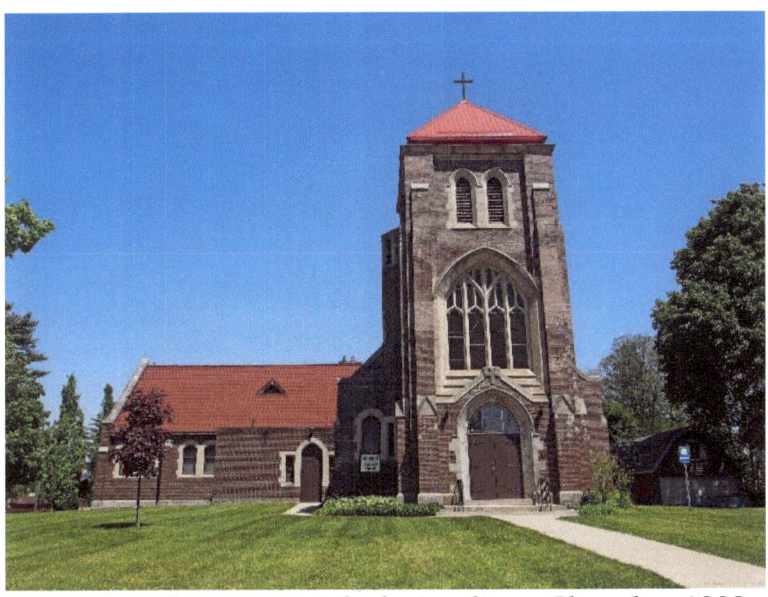

23 Dover Street – St. John's Anglican Church – 1908

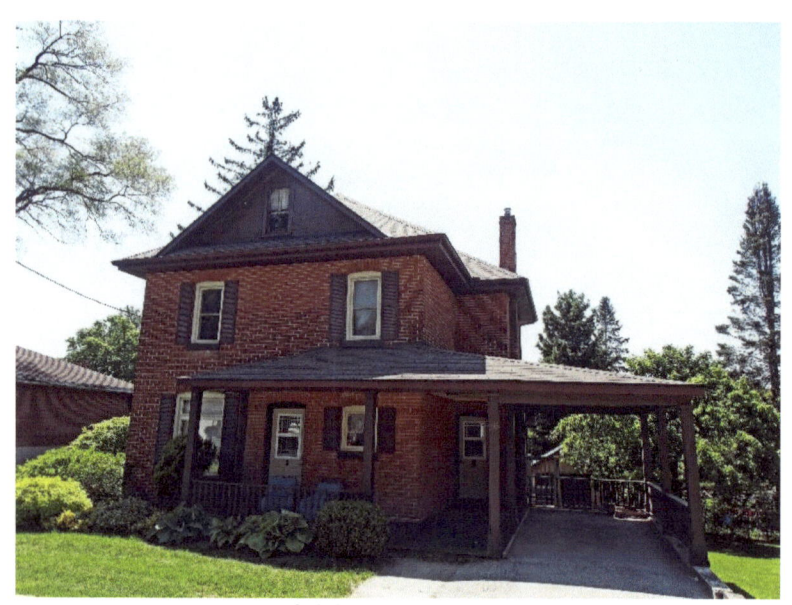
26 Dover Street

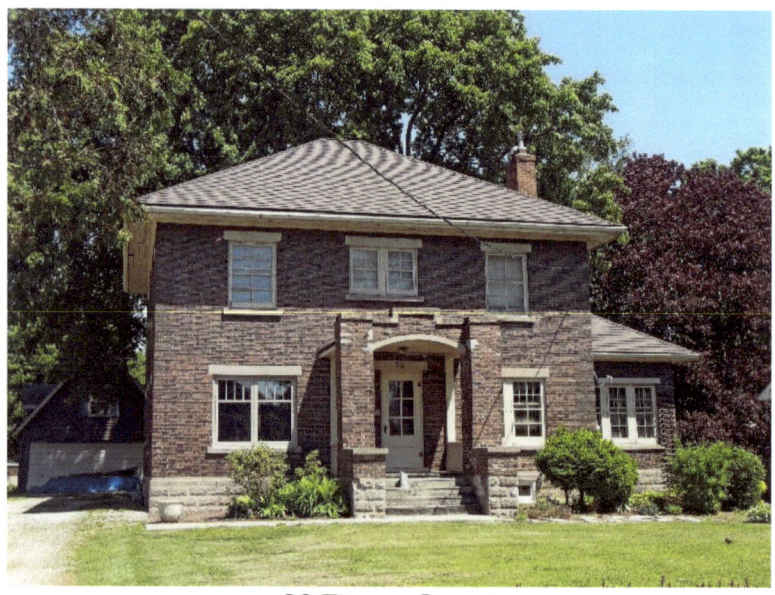
29 Dover Street

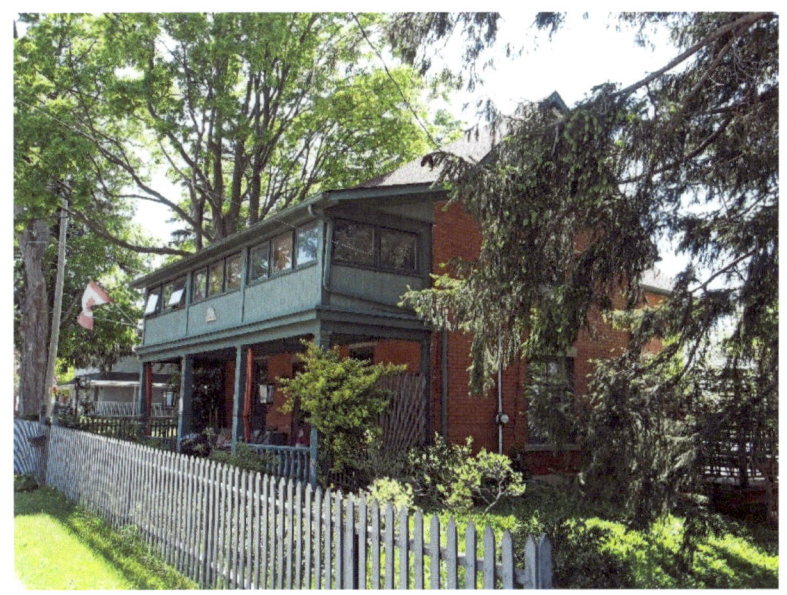

30 Dover Street

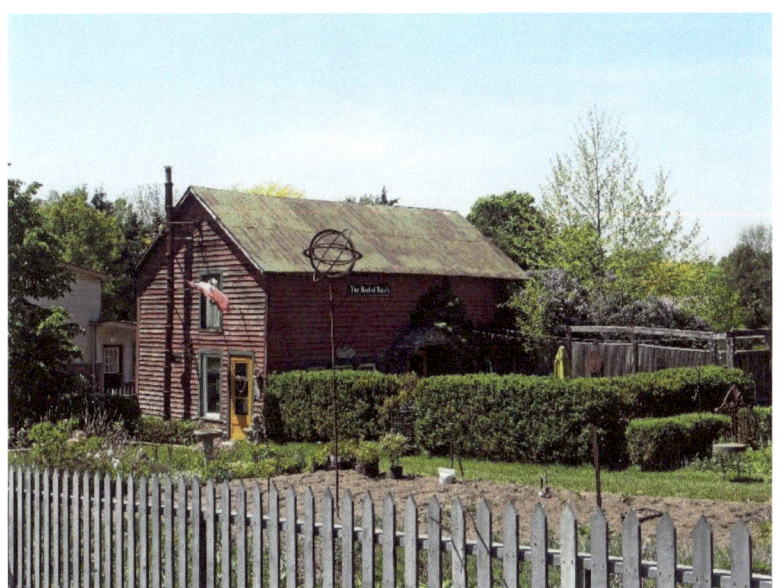

The Herbal Touch

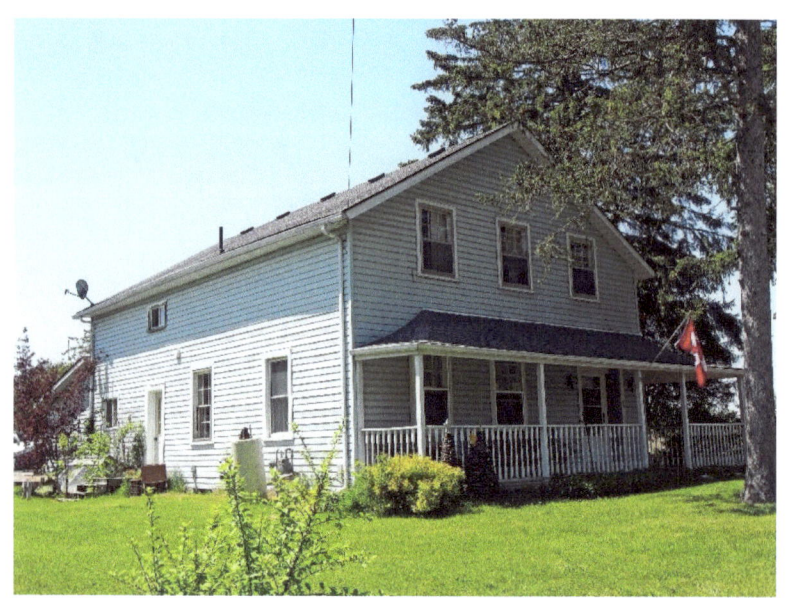
36 Dover Street

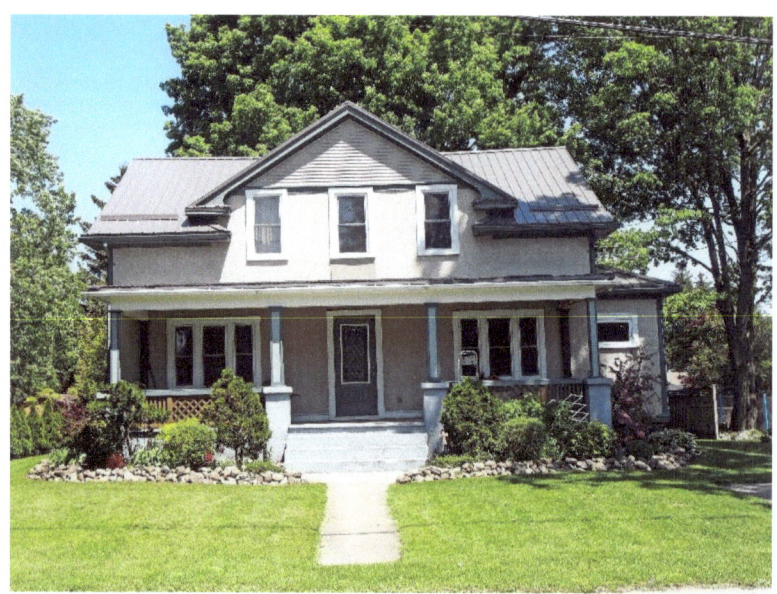
Dover Street

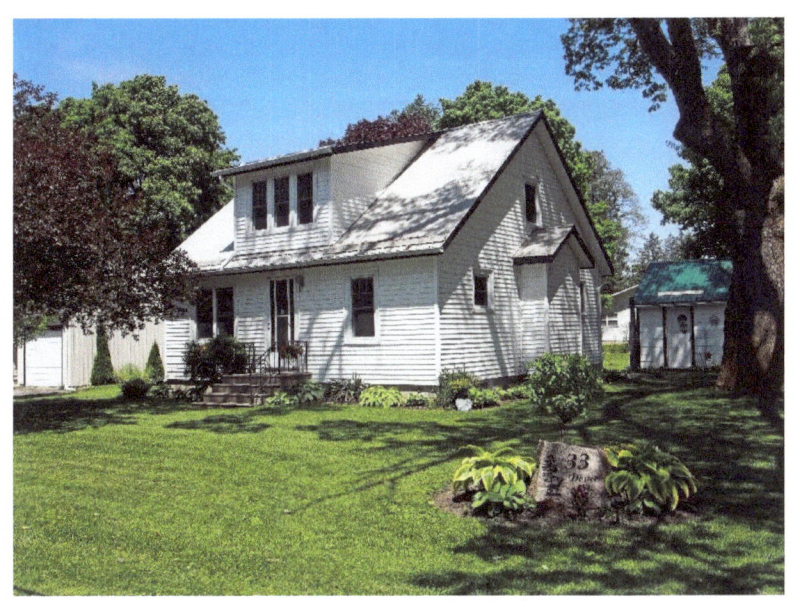

33 Dover Street – shed dormer

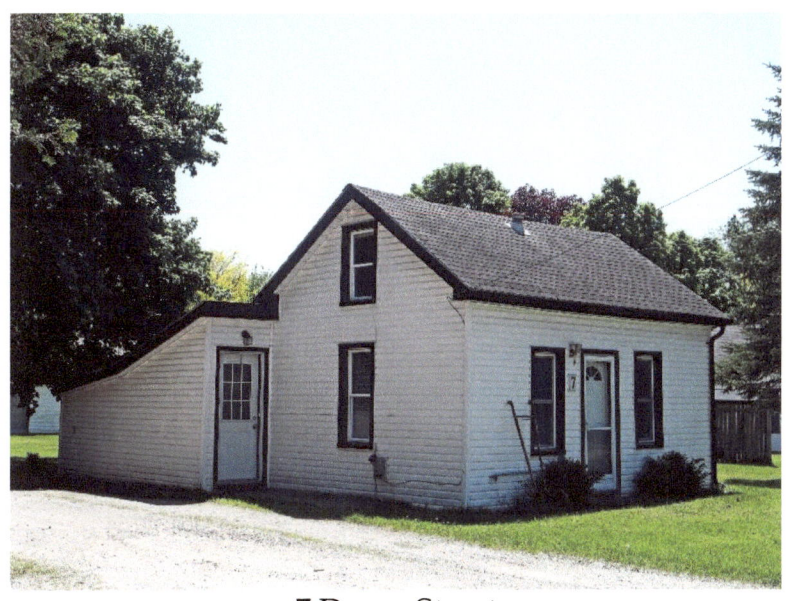

7 Dover Street

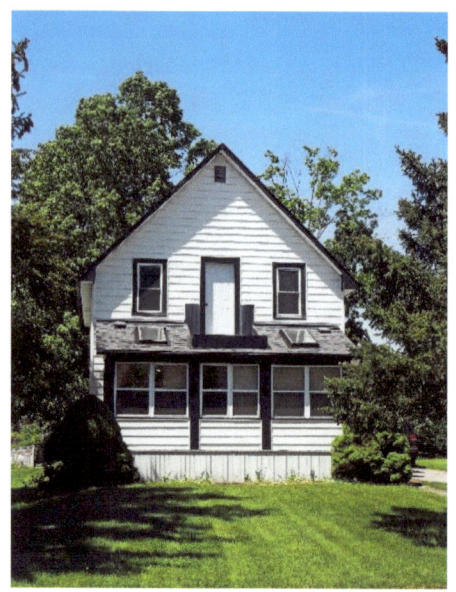
Dover Street

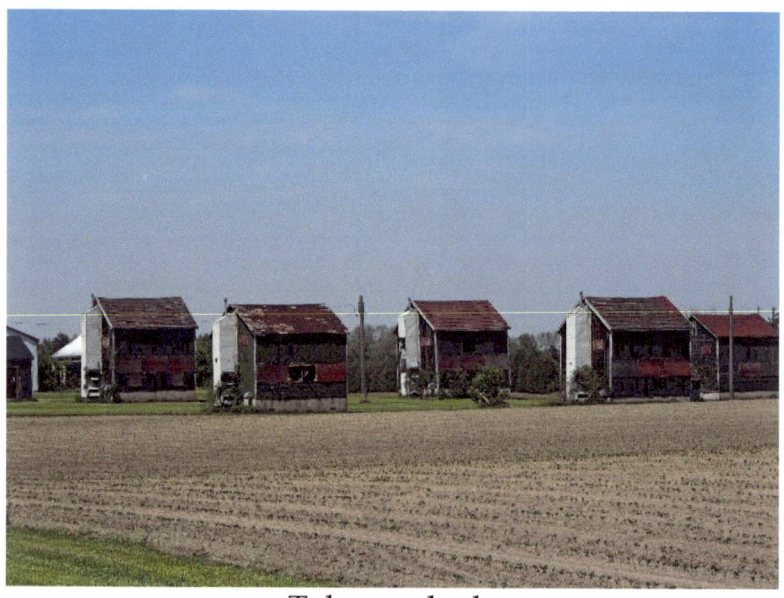
Tobacco sheds

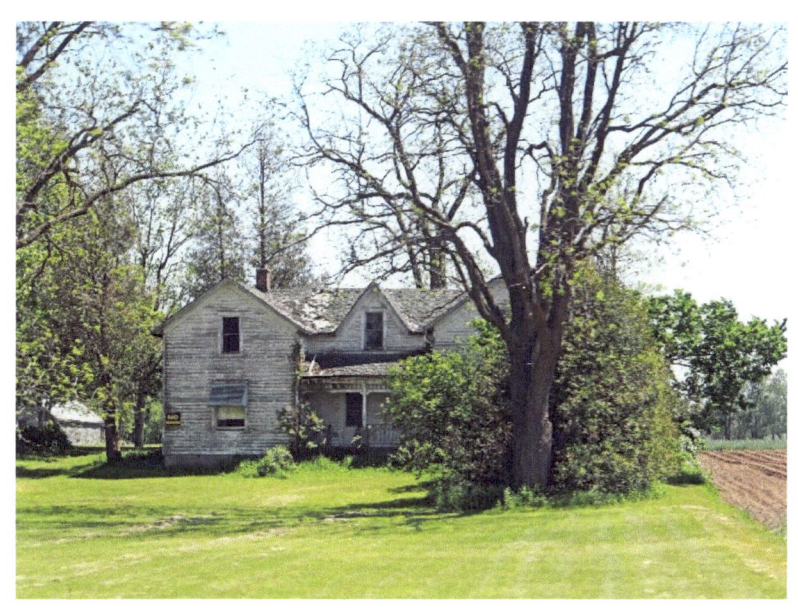

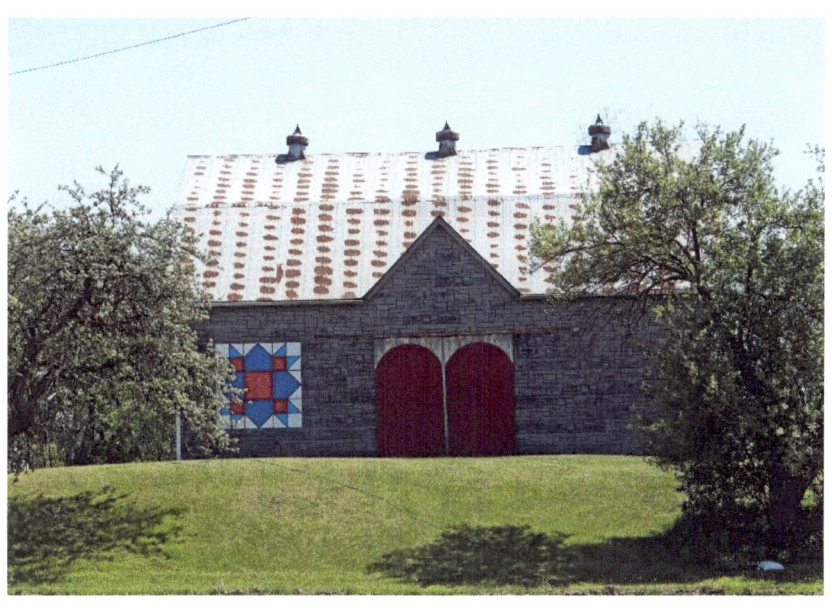

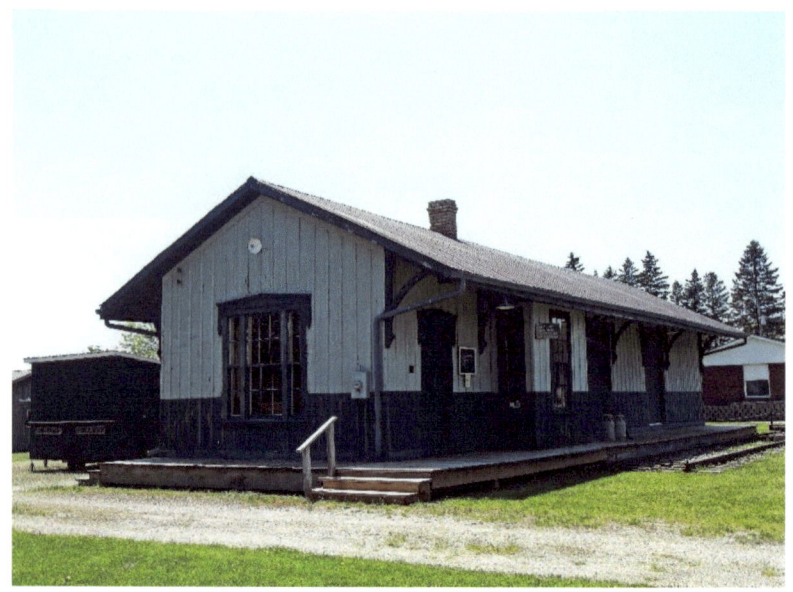

225422 Otterville Road - Otterville South Norwich Historical Society Museum - Grand Trunk Railway Station – 1875 - post and beam construction, with board-and-batten siding, a side gable roof with wide overhanging eaves, supported by prominent eave brackets

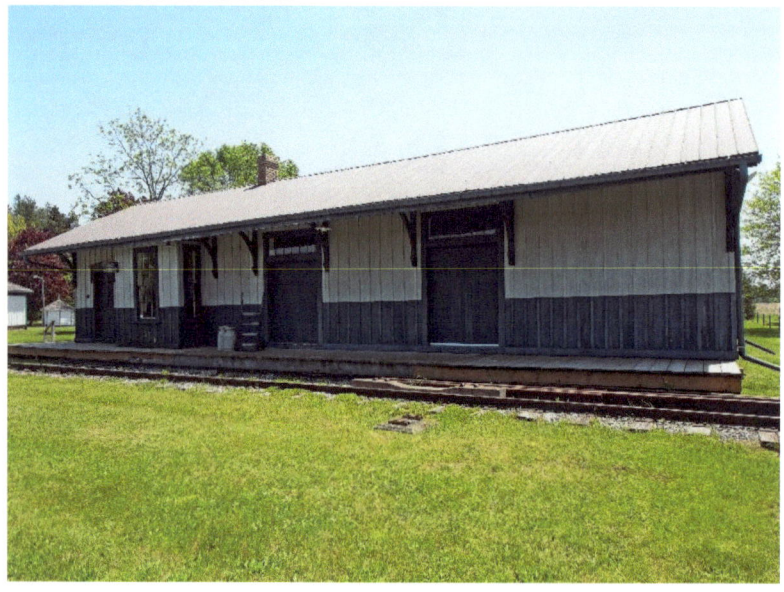

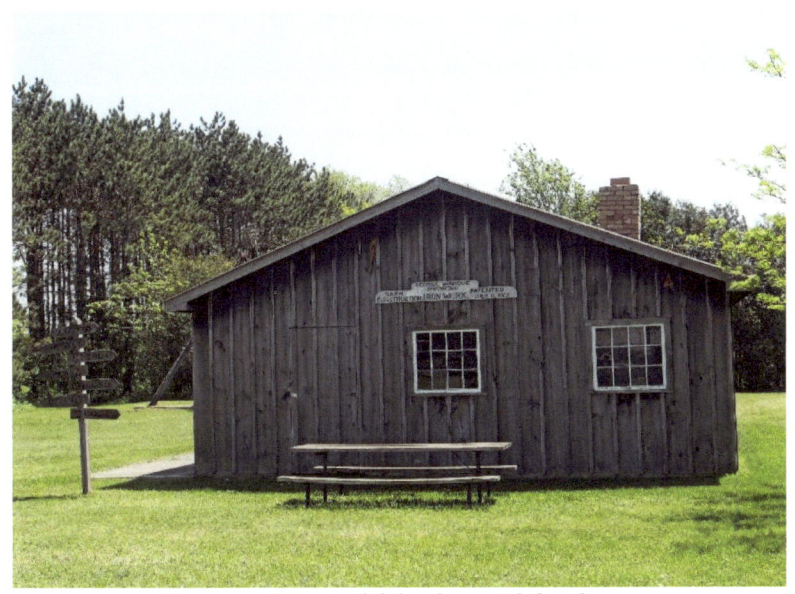
Reconstructed blacksmith's shop

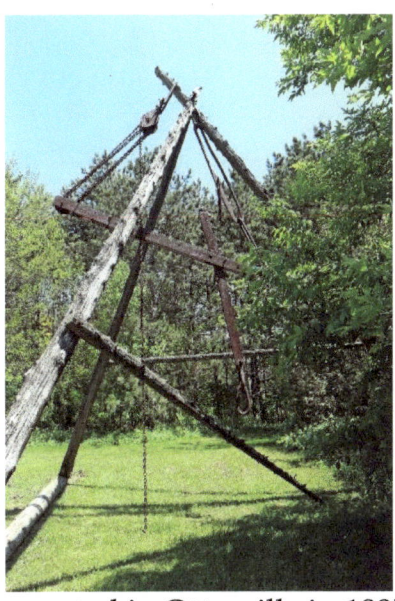
Stump puller invented in Otterville in 1895 by Charles F. Burkholder

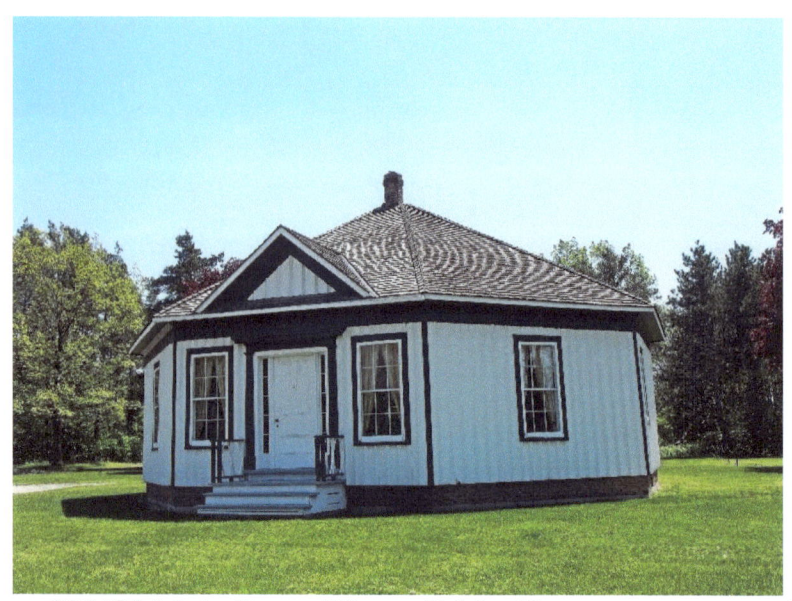

225422 Main Street West - Oddy House - constructed in 1861 – Also called Woodlawn Place which is associated with Thomas Wright, a local, prominent inventor who designed and lived in the building in the mid-nineteenth century. Wright was influenced by Dr. Orson Fowler, whose 1853 book, "The Octagonal House –A Home For All", encouraged the practicality of octagonal dwellings. Fowler argues that these homes were easier to heat and made greater use of the sun's rays.

It is a fine example of the Regency Cottage style of architecture although its octagonal shape makes it unusual. The building is of plank construction with board and batten siding. The overall plan consists of a 45-foot octagon with a 20 foot by 20-foot wing that is situated to form a trapezoidal umbrage at the side of the house. Typical of the Regency style, Woodlawn Place features a wide roof overhang and deep fascia boards. The front door is flanked with sidelights and Doric pilasters, complimented by a simulated entablature above.

Burgessville

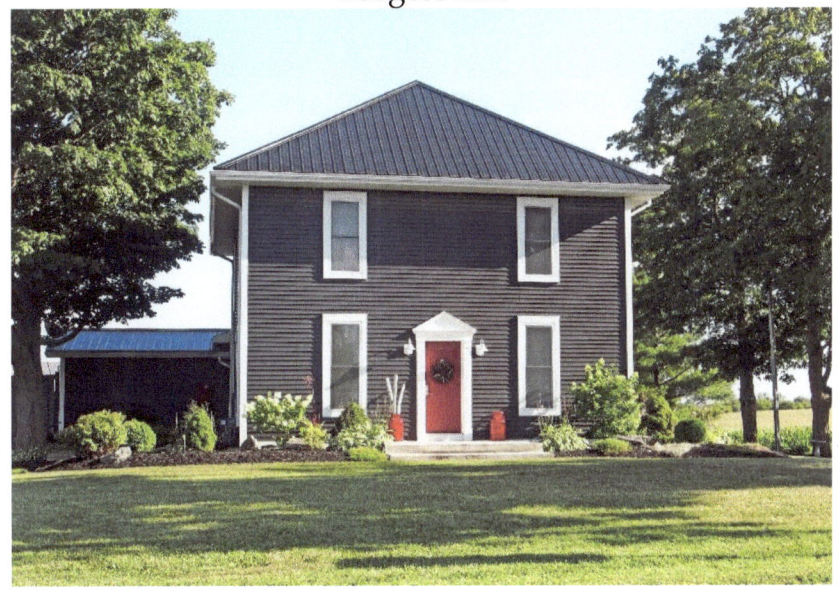

Church Street

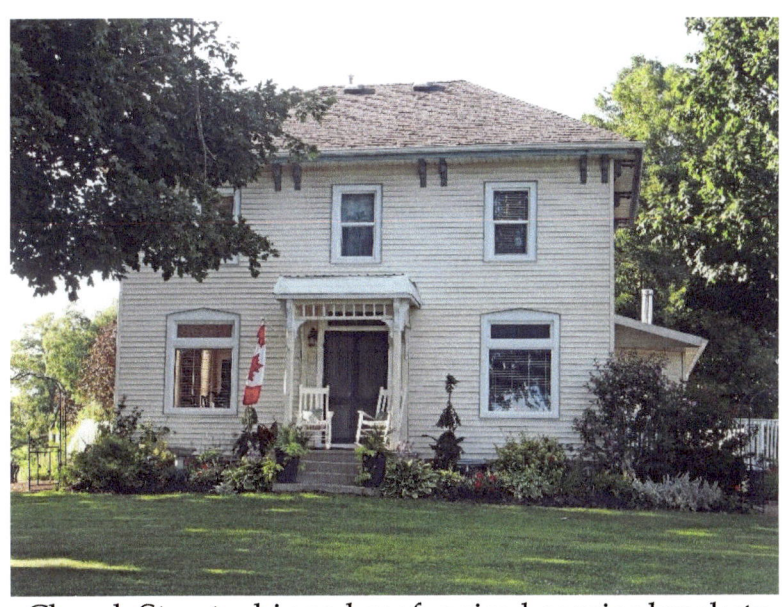

Church Street – hipped roof, paired cornice brackets

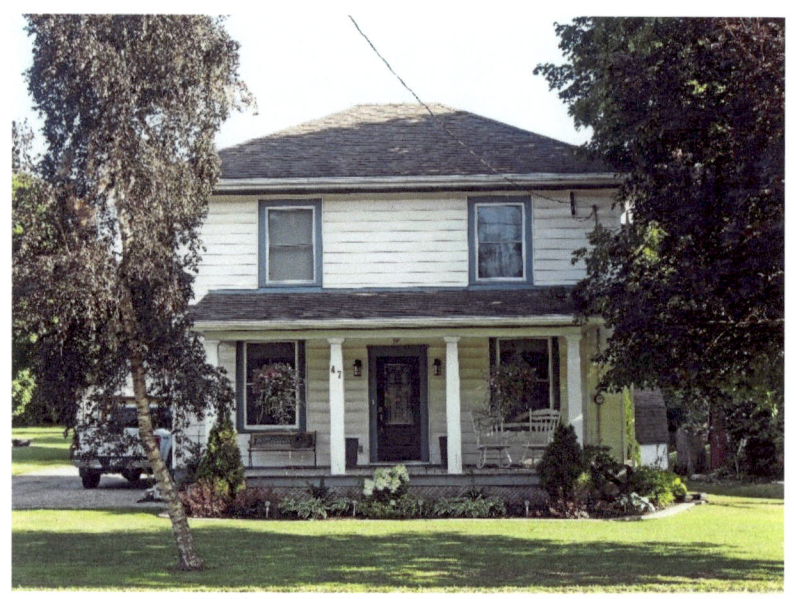
47 Church Street – hipped roof

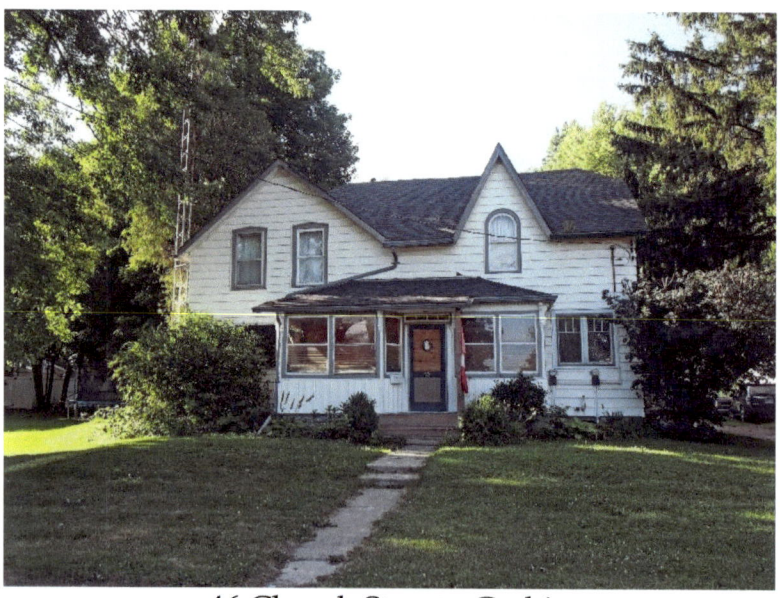
46 Church Street - Gothic

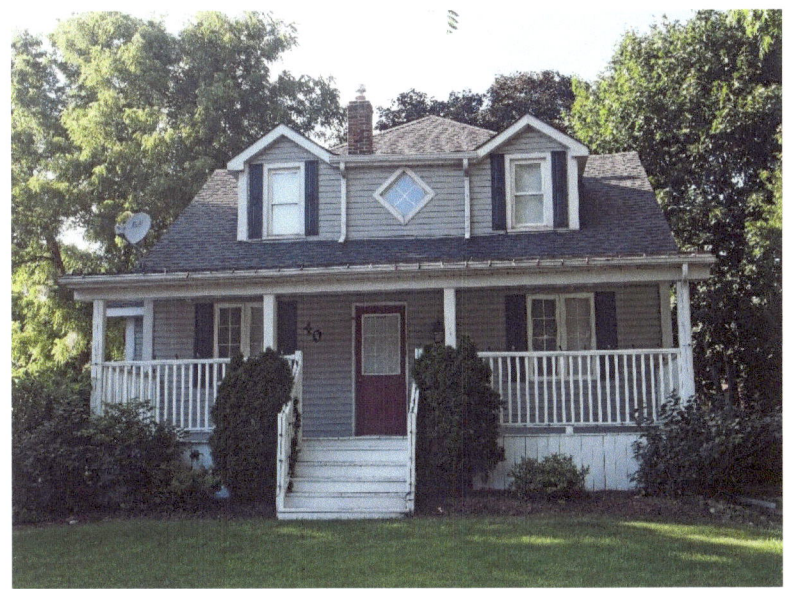

40 Church Street

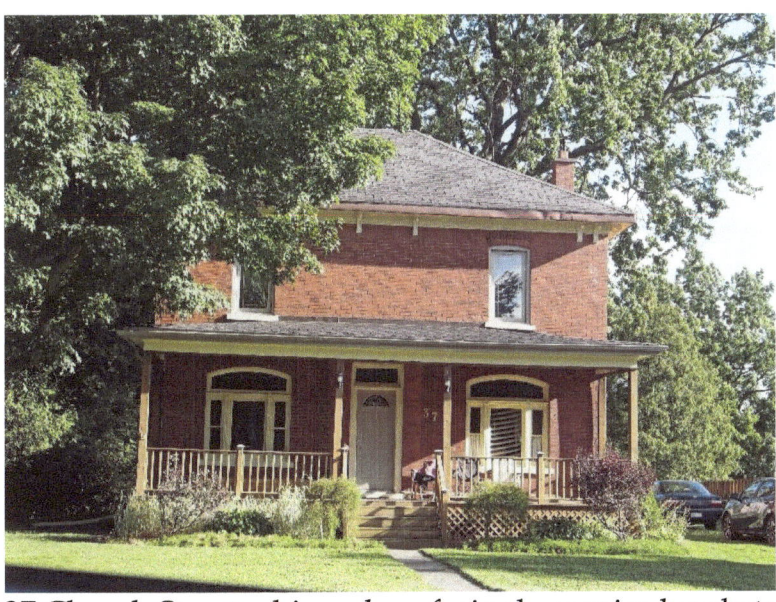

37 Church Street – hipped roof, single cornice brackets

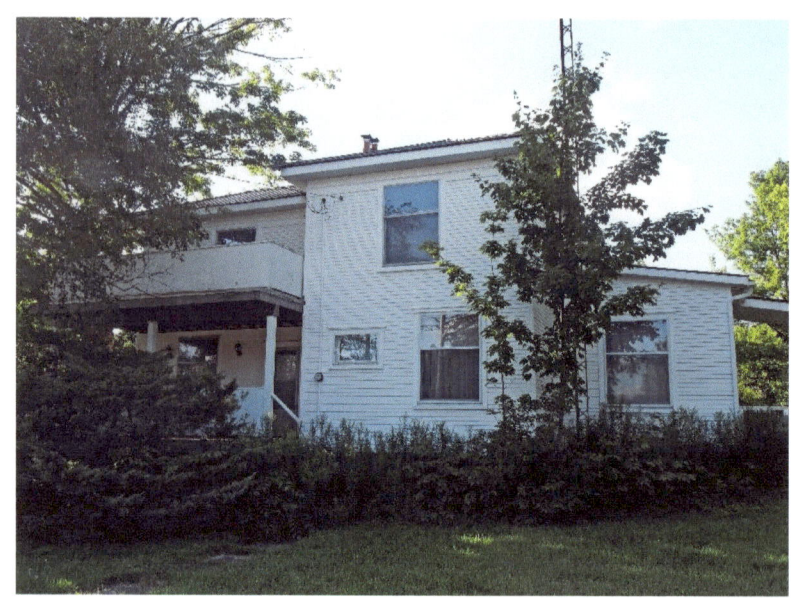
Church Street

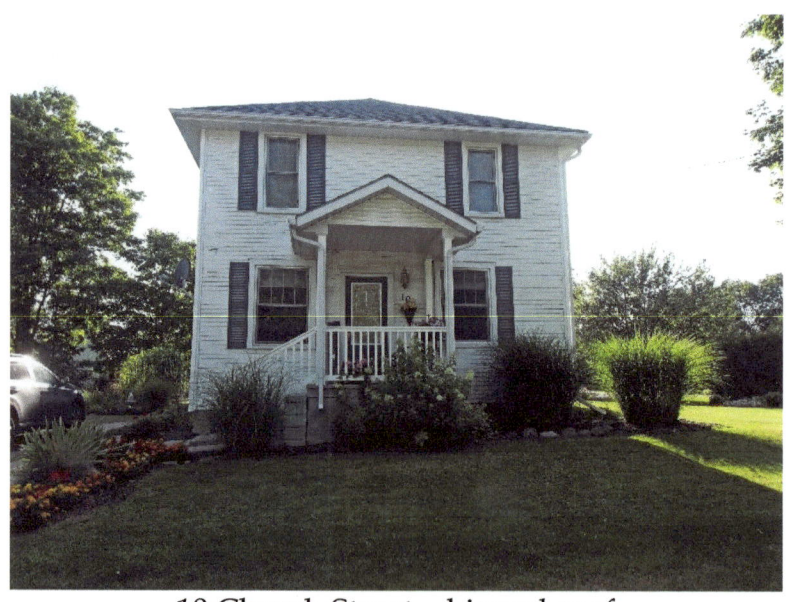
10 Church Street – hipped roof

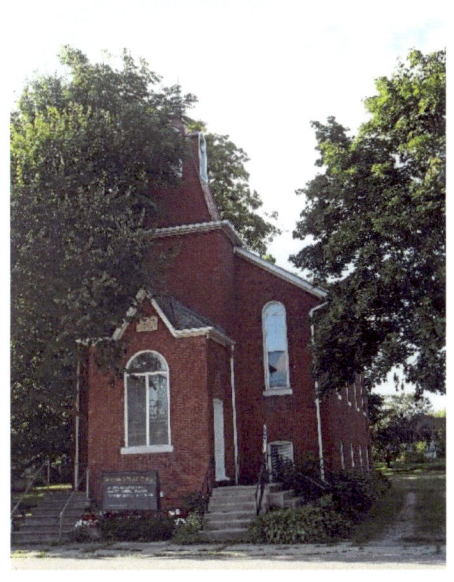

Church Street East – Burgessville United Church

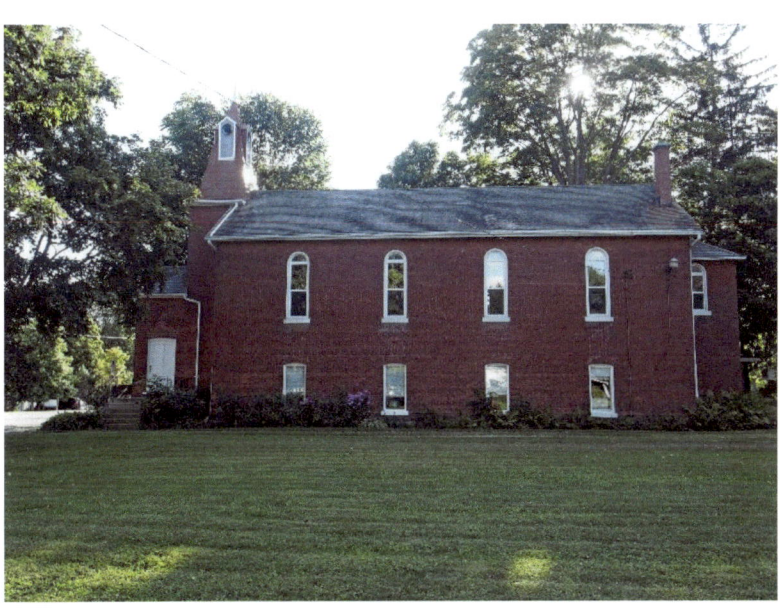

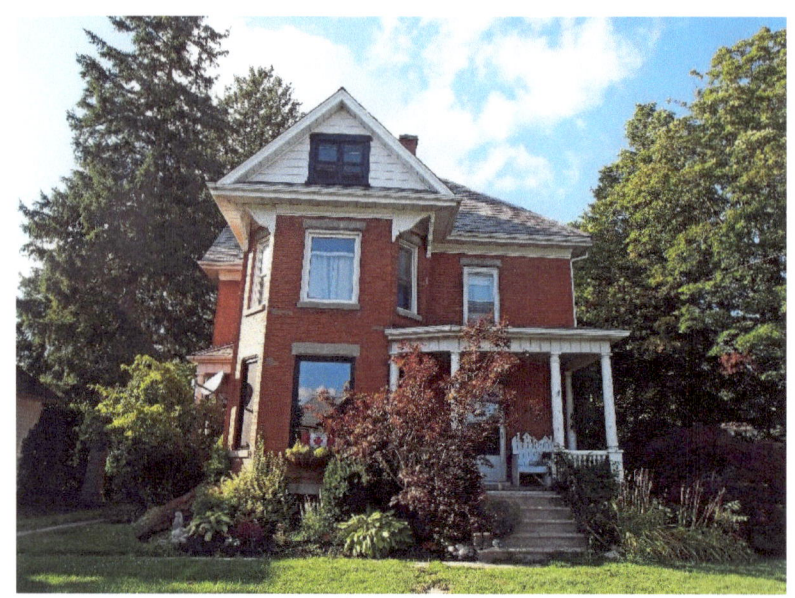
20 Church Street

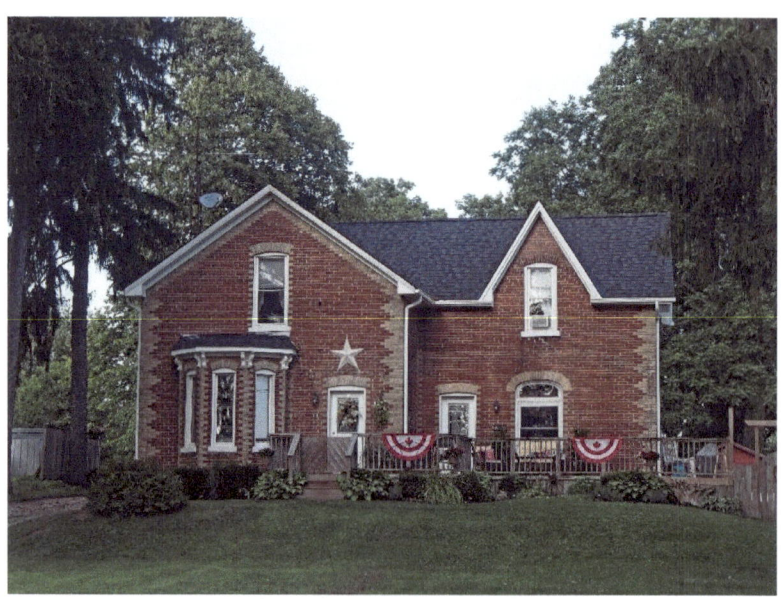
Church Street - Gothic

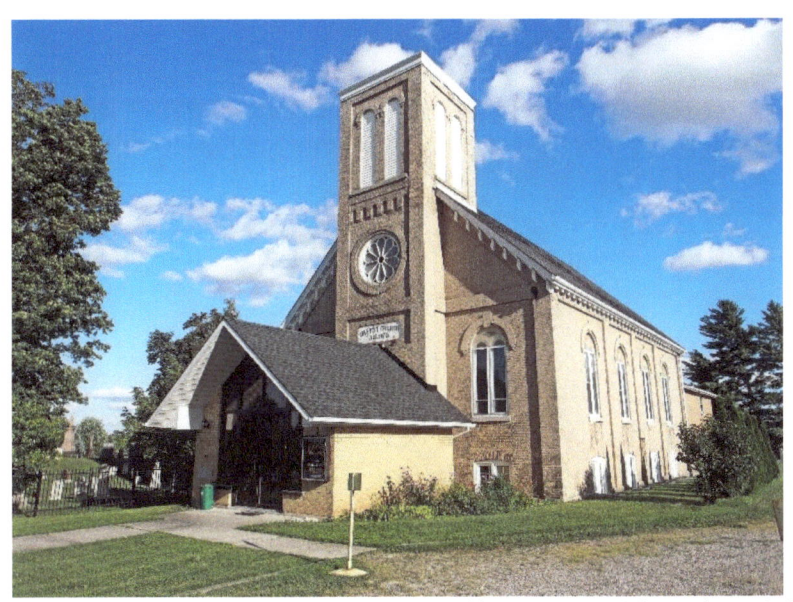

63 Church Street West – Burgessville Baptist Church – A.D. 1870 – rose window

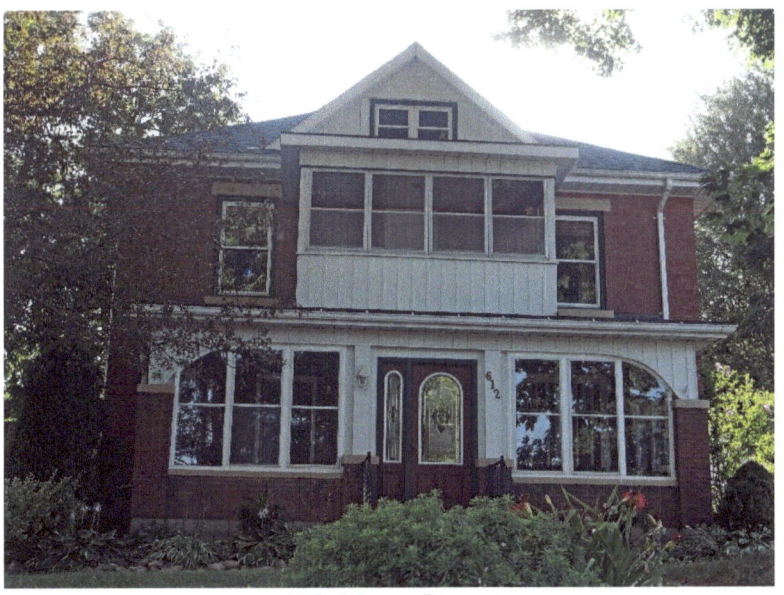

612 Main Street

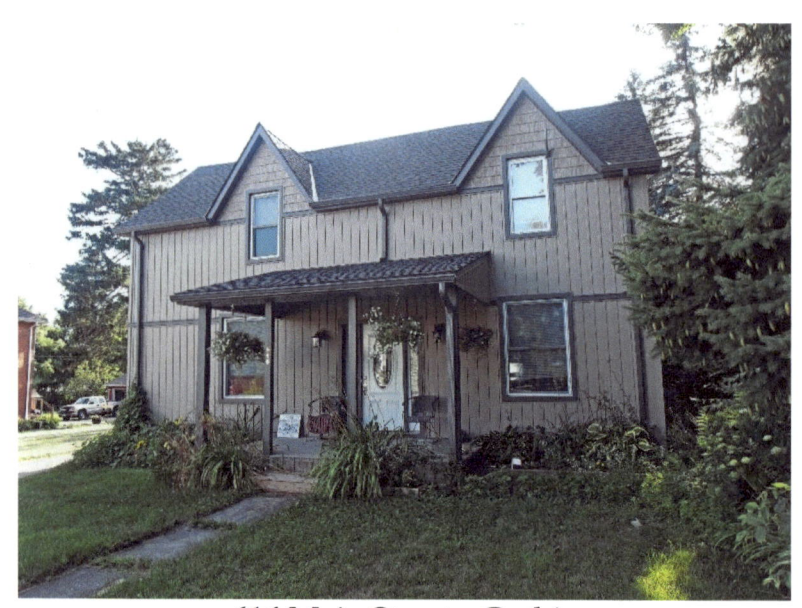

616 Main Street - Gothic

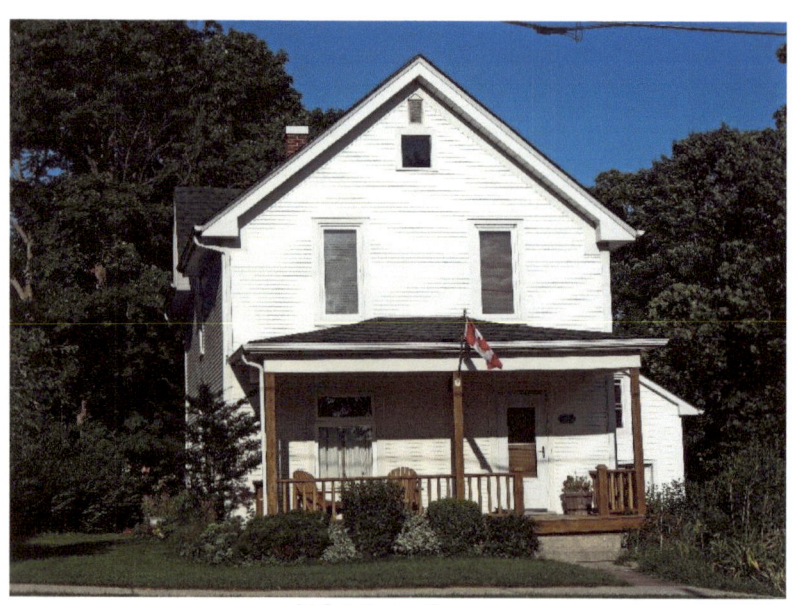

619 Main Street

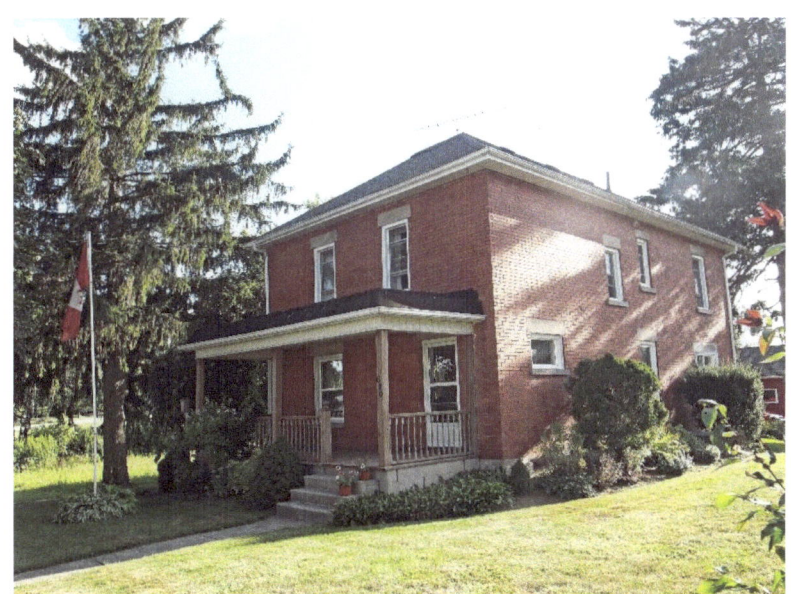

620 Main Street

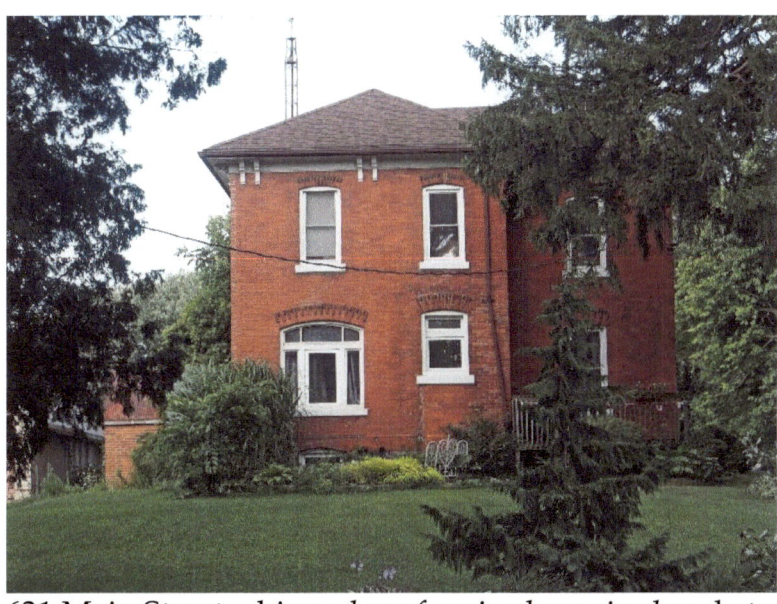

631 Main Street – hipped roof, paired cornice brackets, voussoirs

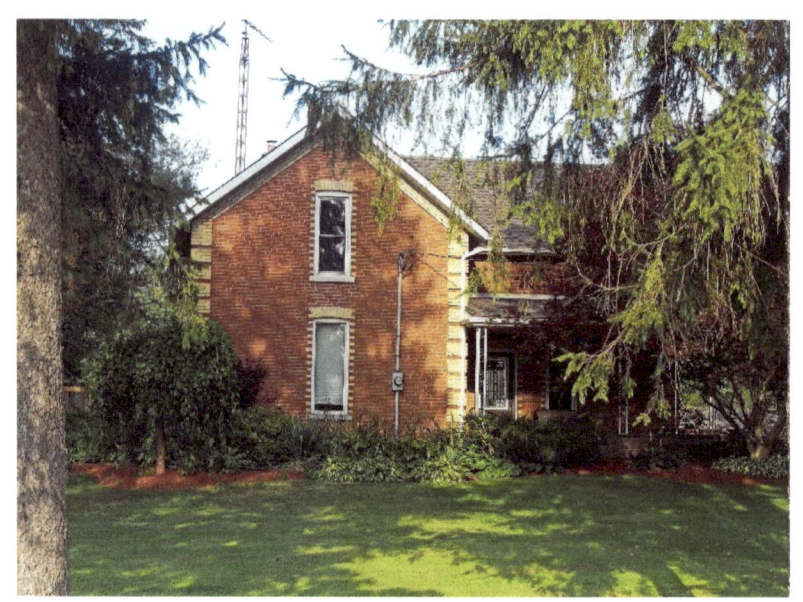
Main Street – corner quoins

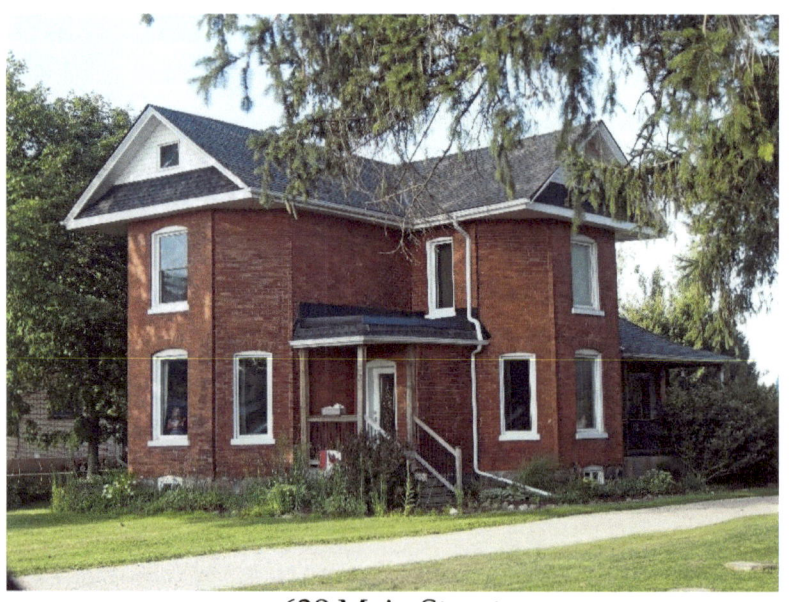
639 Main Street

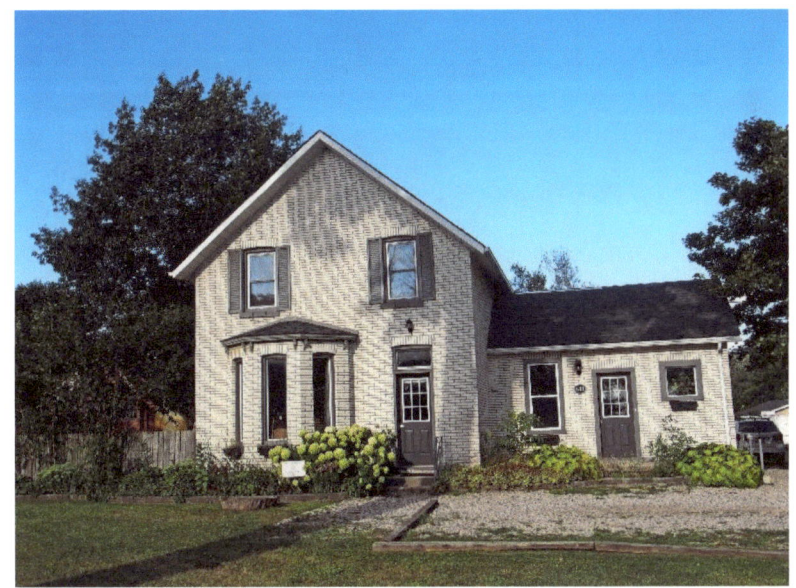

641 Main Street

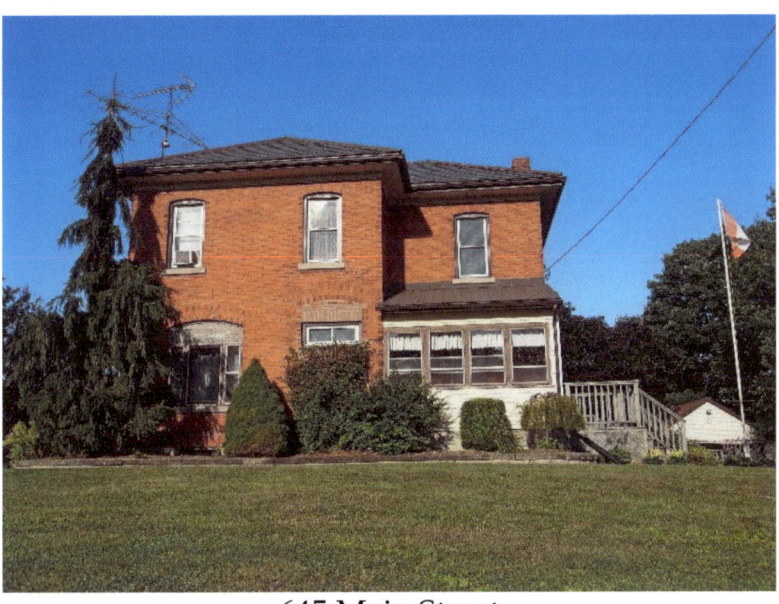

645 Main Street

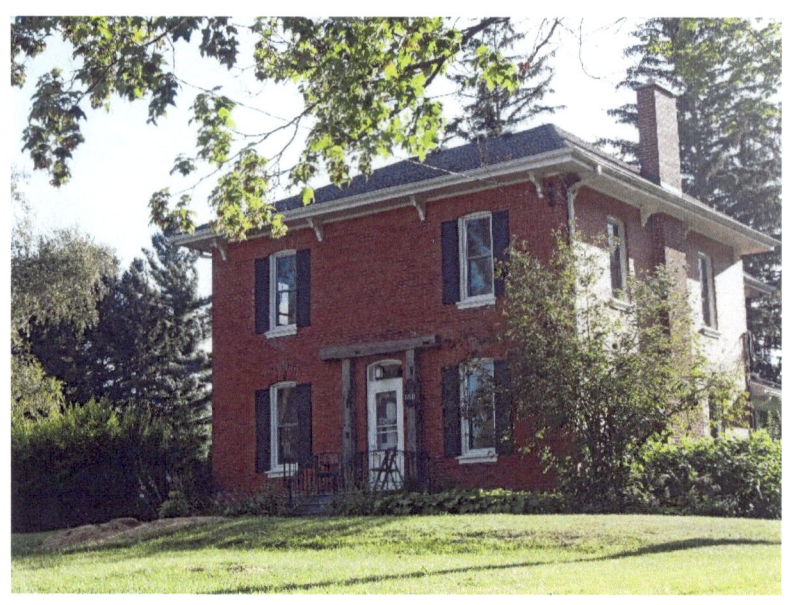

650 Main Street – hipped roof, single cornice brackets, shutters

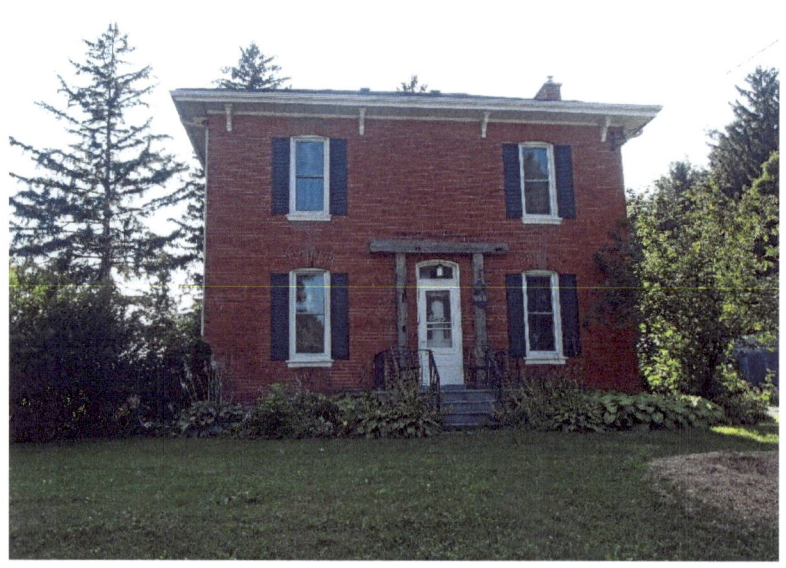

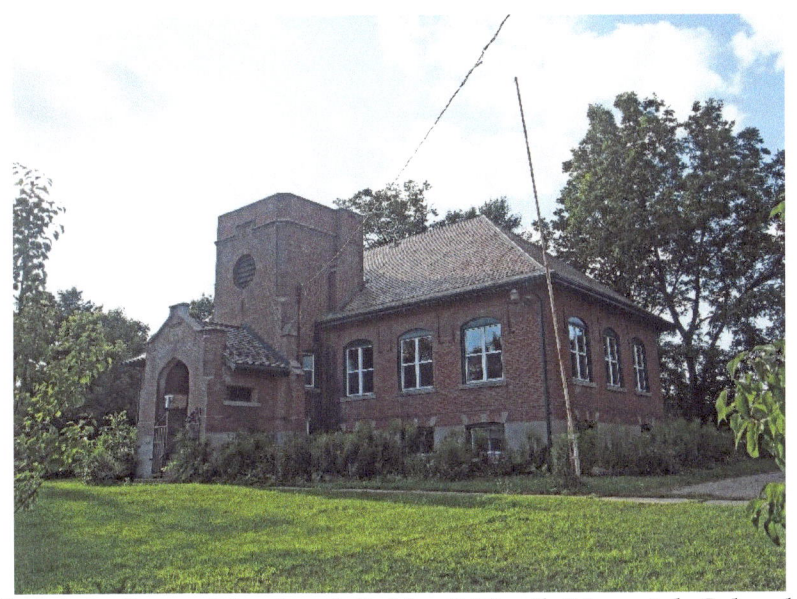

656 Main Street North – S.S. No. 3 North Norwich School – 1905

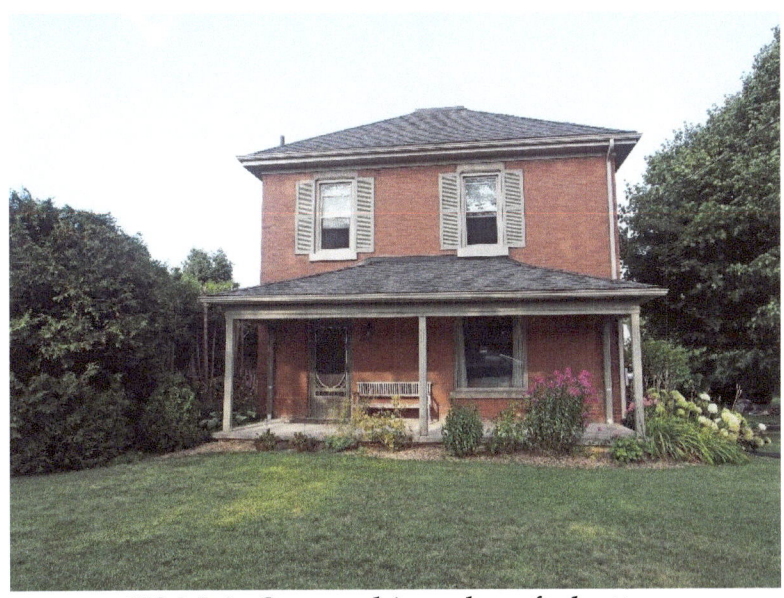

659 Main Street – hipped roof, shutters

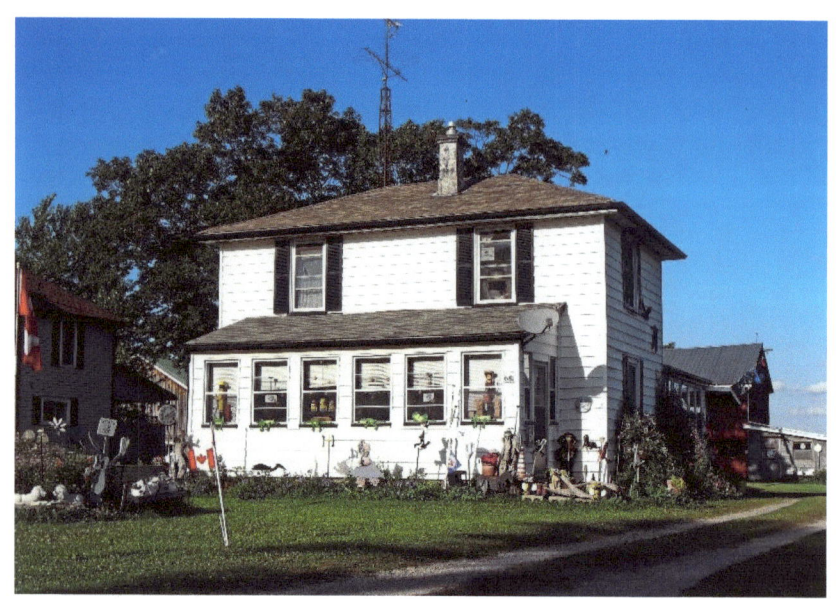

681 Main Street

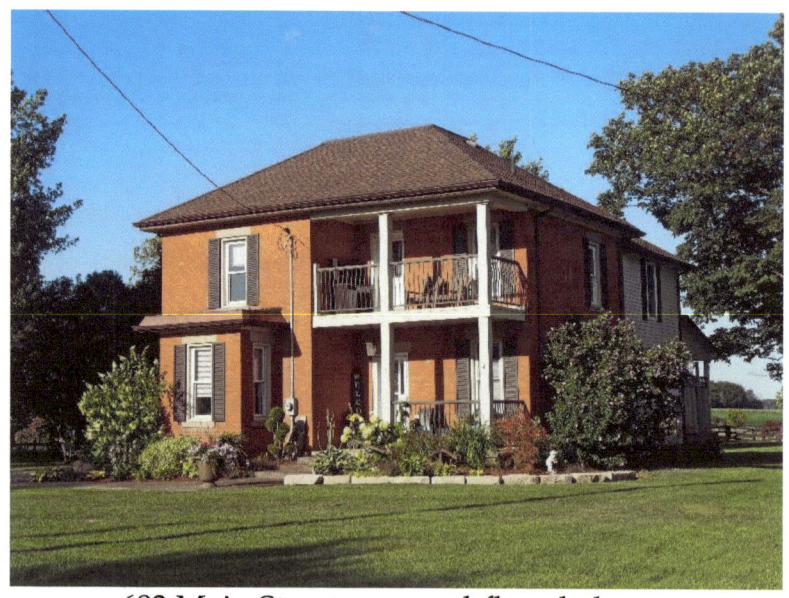

683 Main Street – second-floor balcony

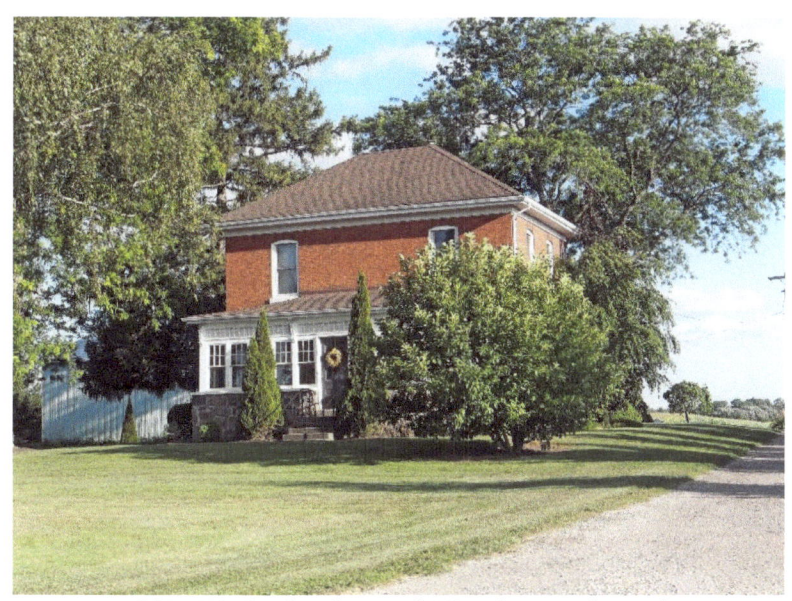

385470 Oxford Road 59 – hipped roof

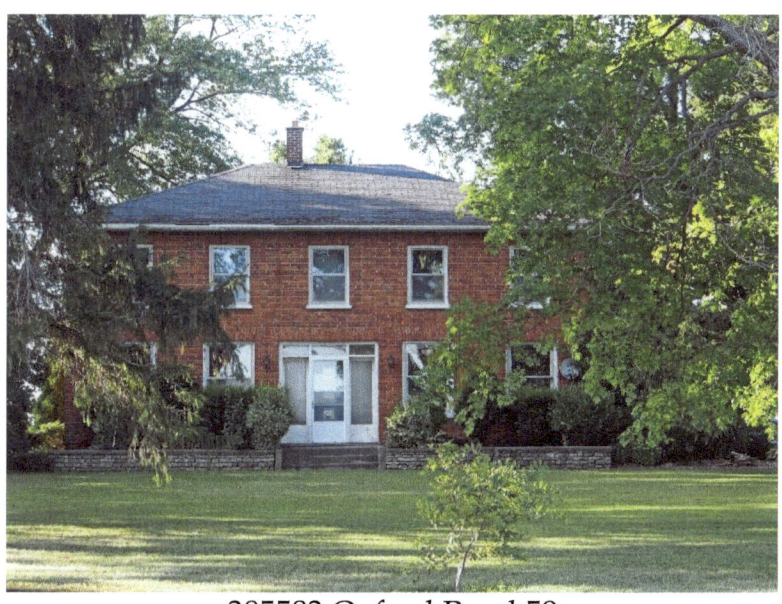

385583 Oxford Road 59

Other Books by Barbara Raue

Coins of Gold
Arrows, Indians and Love
The Life and Times of Barbara
The Cromwell Family Book
Laura Secord Discovered
Daddy Where Are You?

Montana Series
Book 1: Montana Dream
Book 2: Life on the Montana Frontier
Book 3: Montana to Boston and Back
Book 4: Montana Sons Go to War
Book 5: Montana Sons Return from War

© 2019 by Barbara Raue - All the photos in this book have been taken with my cameras. I own the rights to them.

www.ingramcontent.com/pod-product-compliance
Lightning Source LLC
Chambersburg PA
CBHW040237220526
45473CB00001B/281